Living
with
Early
Oak

Living
with
Early
Oak

Seventeenth-Century English Furniture
Then and Now

John Fiske and Lisa Freeman

THE BELMONT PRESS
BELMONT, VERMONT

To Matthew Fiske
1970-2003

Too short a life, dammit.

ISBN: 0-9754569-0-3

The Belmont Press
PO Box 270
Belmont, Vermont 05730
802.259.2579
802.259.3065 fax
info@fiskeandfreeman.com
www.fiskeandfreeman.com

Contents

List of Sidebars   vii
Timeline   ix
Preface   xiii

Part I: When Antiques Were New

Chapter 1: Culture and Lifestyle   3
Chapter 2: The Guild System   22
Chapter 3: Decoration and Style   37

Part II: Forms and Functions

Chapter 4: Storage   61
     Boxes   61
     Coffers   65
     Chests of Drawers   68
     Press Cupboards   74
     Food Storage   79
Chapter 5: Seating   87
     Joint Stools   87
     Wainscot Chairs   90
     Backstools   96
     Benches or Forms   103
     Settles   105
     Turner's Chairs   110
Chapter 6: Tables   117
     Long   117
     Gate-leg   122
     Small   125
Chapter 7: Serving and Display   134
     Court Cupboards   134
     Low Dressers   141
Chapter 8: Beds   149
     Tester   153
     Half-headed   157
     Truckle   157

Part III: An Owner's Handbook

Chapter 9: Restoration and Repairs   165
Chapter 10: The Victorian Goths   175
Chapter 11: Provenance and Patina   183
Chapter 12: Care, Maintenance and Investment   187

Glossary
References
Index

Sidebars

Elizabethan Houses   7
Dining (and Living) in the Hall   12
Trees and People   26
A Turner's Mural Cupboard   31
Caryatids   40
A Late Seventeenth-Century Mannerist Cupboard   43
Panels   44
A Tale of Two Boxes and One Maker   52
A Vernacular Masterwork   56
A Sophisticated Masterwork   57
The Survival Factor   73
Close Stools   90
"The Curious and Ingenious Art and
    Mystery of Japaning"   98
A Farmhouse Winged Armchair   104
Samuel Pepys Throws a Dinner Party   124
A National Style   142
Beds Royal and Humble   151
Bedding and Bed Chambers I   152
Bedding and Bed Chambers II   153
Bedding the Great Bed   155
Reflection   160
To Buy or Not to Buy, that is the Question   168
Fashionable Gothic   176
Patina and Preference   185

Timeline

All timelines risk implying a false precision to the beginnings and endings of cultural trends. This one is no exception. The dates in it should be taken as indicative of mainstream taste: examples of forms or of decoration will be found before and after the dates given, particularly after: trends begin and spread relatively quickly but peter out slowly and unevenly. The dates do not identify specific years but are the center of a roughly five-year span. This timeline should not be used to date specific pieces of furniture, though it may help to determine if a piece is early or late in its period.

TUDOR (Henry VIII 1491-1547, Edward IV 1547-1553, Mary 1553-1558)

1500	Linenfold and simple Parchemin panels become popular.
1520	Romayne panels appear.
1536	Dissolution of the Monasteries begins.
1540	Simple Parchemin panels become enriched.
1560	Linenfold, Romayne, Parchemin panels decline.

ELIZABETHAN (Elizabeth 1558-1603)

1560	The carving of turned legs and posts becomes popular.
	Caryatids and Atlantes coming in.
	Grotesques coming in.
	Roseaces coming in.
1565	Bulbous melon or cup-and-cover leg on tables, court cupboards, and beds becoming fashionable.
1570	Architectural inlay appears on furniture.
	Fluted pilasters appear.
	Cabuchon bosses appear.
	Strapwork carving appears.
	Bible and writing boxes made from now until c. 1700.
1580	Guilloche and Roseace carving fashionable until c. 1640, but used to c. 1700.
	Open court cupboards appear.
	Walnut used for some high class furniture.
1595	Mahogany discovered by Sir Walter Raleigh.
1600	Lozenge carving appears.

Panel back chairs acquire cresting.
Scalloping the lower edge of seat rails on joint stools and wainscot chairs becomes popular.

JACOBEAN (James I 1603-1625, Charles I 1625-1648)

1610	Farthingale chairs appear.
1620	A few upholstered chairs and stools made for court and aristocracy.
1630	Caryatids and Atlantes decline.
	Strapwork declines.
	Inlay declines.
	Scalloping on the lower side of joint stool rails and front seat rails of wainscot chairs declines.
1635	Enclosed chests of drawers appear.
	Spiral turnings appear, become popular c. 1660.
	Lozenge very fashionable.
1640	Guilloche and Roseace go out of fashion, but are still found until c. 1700 especially in the north.
	Applied split-balusters and moldings appear.
	Pearl and bone inlay appears.
	Boarded ends replace paneled ends on coffers.
	"Cromwellian" chairs appear.

COMMONWEALTH or CROMWELLIAN (1648-1659)

1650	Carving discouraged, figural carving disappears.
	Backstools become popular, particularly in the north, until c. 1700.
	Ball, or bobbin, and ball-and-ring turnings appear.
	Leather-upholstered chairs appear.

RESTORATION or CAROLEAN (Charles II 1660-1685, James II 1685-1689)

1660	Draw tables no longer made.
	Carving on bedsteads declining.
	Gate-leg tables popular, long tables declining.
	Spiral turnings popular.
	Caning on chair seats and backs becomes fashionable.
	Applied decorations (bosses, split balusters, moldings) in high fashion.
	Turned wooden pulls on drawers .
	Flat stretchers become fashionable, especially on small tables.
	Bun feet appear.
1665	Cromwellian chairs replaced by high-backed caned chairs, usually in

walnut, until c. 1700.

Pendants replace turned supports on top tier of press cupboards.

1666   Great Fire of London destroyed 13,000 houses and their contents. Continental craftsmen were allowed in, and London became the furniture manufacturing center of the western world.

1670   Ball, and ball-and-ring turnings decline.

Loop drop handles decline.

"Restoration" chairs with crowns or crown and cupids in fashion.

Chests of drawers become popular, replacing coffers, particularly in the south.

Applied geometric moldings standard decoration for drawer-fronts, and some panels on chests and doors.

Low dressers appear.

S-scroll decoration popular until c. 1700.

1675   Double S-scroll leg appears.

Marquetry appears.

1680   Serpentine stretchers, often of X-form, appear.

Baluster-turned stiles on chair backs.

Applied split-bobbin molding popular until 1700.

Oyster veneering become popular.

Candlestands appear.

1685   Upholstered wing chairs appear.

Pearl and bone inlay declines.

WILLIAM & MARY (William and Mary 1689-1702; Mary died 1695, William III 1695-1702)

1690   Ebonized bosses declining.

Octagonal legs appear.

Flat stretchers decline.

Bracket feet appear.

Desks, or bureaus, appear.

Seaweed pattern in marquetry becomes fashionable.

Fiddle splats appear.

1695   Cabriole legs appear.

Ball and claw feet appear.

"Hoop back" or Queen Anne chair backs begin to replace tall-backs.

Cupped legs fashionable.

Hoof feet begin 10-year period of fashion.

1700   Caning declines.

Bracket feet dominant on case pieces.

Knee-hole desks appear.

Hooded and broken pediments appear.

1700   Console tables appear.
        Tall boys, chests on stands, appear.
        Seventeenth-century carving disappears.
        Daybeds, coffers, paneled-back chairs disappear.
        Bible boxes and writing slopes decline.

Preface

Where this Book Comes From

This book has twin roots, one in our experience as dealers and the other in our previous lives in universities.

It has grown out of hundreds of conversations with our customers. It is a book about what people want to know about seventeenth century oak furniture:

- what it is and why it is the way that it is;
- how people lived with it then, and how they might use it today;
- what to look out for when buying it; and
- how to look after it in the home.

The fact that we deal in English furniture in America (and, incidentally, that John is English and Lisa American) has shaped these conversations and questions: Americans will, inevitably, ask some questions that the English won't. This transatlantic perspective is also an integral part of our own thinking, and we believe that it gives this book a different tone from most books on English furniture.

While we are dealers in early oak, we also live with it. Early oak furniture is part of our lives, and not merely a commodity in which we trade. We collected it, ate off it, and furnished with it long before we dealt in it. We have centered this book around what we might call "everyday oak," that is, the furniture with which "middling folk" furnished their homes, rather than the special pieces of the court and aristocracy. This honest, sturdy furniture is as appropriate to the people who use it now as it was to its original owners.

The second root was planted in the university world. Before becoming full-time antique dealers, we were both involved in the discipline of cultural studies and material culture, John as a professor and author, and Lisa as a publisher. Cultural studies is based upon a simple premise: every society produces things that enable its members to live comfortably. These objects are specific to that society, and can provide rich insights into the lives of the people who live with them. They are, literally, living things. Cultural studies teaches us that objects as ordinary as tables and chairs are as significant as Shakespeare.

In this book, then, we bring together the three essentials for getting the most pleasure from early oak furniture:

• We admire its beauty and strength and analyze the distinctiveness of both its appearance and its construction.

• We celebrate its usefulness, both then when it was new, and now when it is antique.

• We read it as documents written in oak that give us insights into where we came from.

Overall, then, we aim to show how form, function and history illuminate each other, and to encourage the reader to see all three dimensions simultaneously.

The Organization of the Book

Living with Early Oak is divided into three parts.

Part I: When Antiques Were New is an account of seventeenth-century domestic life as we can read it in its furniture. It treats furniture as historical documents that are simultaneously the products and the records of peoples' lifestyles.

Part II: Forms and Functions describes the main forms of seventeenth-century furniture that are available to today's collectors. It gives glimpses of how they were lived with then, when they were new, and how they can be lived with now, when they are antique.

Part III: An Owners' Handbook is a practical manual for today's collectors. It offers advice on what to look out for when buying early oak, and on how to look after it in the home.

At the back of the book readers will find a Glossary and References.

Language and Jargon

Language changes, but things do not. Therein lies a problem. The same piece of furniture has been called many different names over its lifetime, and still is. In each case we familiarize our readers with all the names they might meet, while preferring one as the most accurate and useful.

Technical processes and details have specialist names – jargon, as it is often called. When well used, jargon clarifies our understanding: when used badly it muddies it. We have tried to use it sparingly and well. We have explained it as we use it and have added a glossary at the end of the book. You can't understand anything properly without understanding the language that experts use when they talk about it.

There is one small group of jargon words that is so fundamental and elementary that you can't start reading the book if you don't understand them. They are joined (including joiner, joinery, joint), mortise-and-tenon, panel, and, finally, rail, stile, and muntin.

A joiner makes furniture by using a mortise-and-tenon joint to join two boards at right angles. All joined furniture depends upon one basic structure: a rectangular frame made of four boards mortise-and-tenoned together. In storage (or "case") furniture, this frame encloses a panel, which is set in grooves in the inside of the frame. The frame takes the weight, so the panel can be thin. In tables and chairs ("support" furniture), these frames are open and support the tops and seats. Joined and paneled construction uses wood economically, it makes furniture light and easily moveable, and it looks good. It also allows the panel to move with changes in humidity, thus reducing the likelihood of it splitting.

In case furniture the horizontal boards are known as rails, the vertical ones as stiles and muntins. Stiles are load-bearing, usually extending downward as legs; muntins divide and support two adjacent panels. Often the distinction between stile and muntin is unnecessary, in which case we use the word stile to include both.

In support furniture (chairs, stools, tables), the same names apply, but with exceptions: rails are the horizontal boards joining the tops of the legs and supporting the chair seats or table tops (they are often called aprons or friezes.) The bottom rails of the frame, however, are called stretchers. The vertical, load-bearing sides of the frame are called legs, not stiles, except when they extend above the seat to form a chair back. A paneled chair back is formed by two vertical stiles joined by horizontal rails, of which the upper is the crest rail. Legs and stretchers may be turned, except at the joints, which are always left as square blocks for the mortises and tenons.

References and Illustrations

References to modern books are given with the author's name followed by the date of publication and the page number in parentheses. Full details are given in the References at the end.

References to books published in the period are treated similarly. Other period sources, such as inventories or diaries, are often cited by a number of modern authorities. In this case, no modern reference is given. When a source is cited by one modern author only, the author is credited.

Acknowledgments

This book would not have been possible without the research of the furniture historians who have preceded us. We add no new research material but instead recount their results in a different tone of voice for a different reader.

The culmination of this scholarship is Victor Chinnery's definitive book *Oak Furniture: the British Tradition*, but he is the first to acknowledge the work of those who went before him. Most of them are also acknowledged in this book, and their works are listed in the References.

There is another form of scholarship on which we have relied extensively. It is less well documented, but is no less important. Dealers in early oak have handled thousands of pieces, turned them inside out and upside down, and have collectively accumulated an immense body of knowledge. We are grateful to our fellow dealers on both sides of the Atlantic for countless conversations, demonstrations, and cups of tea. If we have to single one out for special thanks, it must be Andrew Singleton of Suffolk House Antiques. Thank you, Andrew, for all your help with both the text and the illustrations.

Victor Chinnery and John Andrews have been particularly generous in allowing us access both to their expertise and to their collections of photographs.

Thanks are also due to Dick Freeman for his eagle eye.

We thank our colleagues in the trade who have helped us with illustrations:

Day Antiques, 5 New Church St, Tetbury, Gloucestershire, GL8 8DS, UK
Malcolm Franklin Antiques, 34 East Oak St, Suite 200, Chicago, IL 60611, USA
Jan and John Maggs Antiques, 2 Old Cricket Hill Rd, Conway, MA 01341, USA
William A. Smith Auctions, Plainfield, NH 03781, USA
George Subkoff Antiques, 230 Post Road East, Westport, CT 06880, USA
Suffolk House Antiques, High St, Yoxford, Suffolk, IP17 3EP, UK.

We are grateful to have been permitted to publish photographs of pieces in private and public collections:

Camcote House Collection
Bob and Sara Hunt Collection
Jud Hartmann Collection
Historic Deerfield, Deerfield, Massachusetts
The Victoria and Albert Museum, London
The British Library, London
Jesus College, Oxford
Museum Boijmans Van Beuningen, Rotterdam
Astley Hall Museum and Art Gallery, Chorley, Lancashire

We are also grateful to those owners who prefer not to be identified and whose collections are acknowledged simply as "Private."

PART I

When Antiques Were New

CHAPTER 1
Culture and Lifestyle

The seventeenth century is a fascinating period: during its span of 125 years (let's stretch it backward a bit to include the end of the sixteenth century), our ancestors changed their social order from a medieval to a modern one. If we could be guests at a meal in Elizabethan or Jacobean England, for example, we would feel completely out of place, not knowing how to behave or even where to sit. By the reign of William and Mary, however, we would feel at home: we would have joined an early modern, and thus recognizable, society, rather than a late medieval one.

As guests at an Elizabethan meal, we would have joined a household of about twenty people. We would have sat on stools along one side of a long table. Only the head of the household, and perhaps his wife, would have sat on a chair: their table would have been at right angles to ours, raised on a dais at the head of the room. Retainers dining with us, or the children, may have sat on benches on the other side of the table. We would have shared drinking glasses and even spoons. Where we sat and what we sat on were rigidly determined by our social standing. We would have been dining in a hierarchy.

At the end of the seventeenth century, eight or ten of us would have sat around an oval gate-leg table, each of us on a similar backstool, and each with our own set of cutlery and wine glass. We would have sat and eaten as individuals with equal rights rather than as ranked subjects in a hierarchy. Our table manners would have changed as much as our seating patterns, our cutlery, and our furniture. At this meal we would have felt modern: at its Elizabethan counterpart we would have felt dislocated and medieval.

Figure 1.1: Medieval dining in France, c. 1475. The signs of status are clear in this meal. The high table is on a dais, and only men are seated at it. The women and lower-ranking men are seated at the lower table on benches built into the wall. The only diner with her back to the room is a woman, and she is seated on a bench, the lowliest form of seating: it is possible that she was a handmaiden. Note how close the diners are sitting to each other, a sign of a society with little sense of personal space. (The wear on the stretchers of the table in figure 6.3 shows that six people sat along a side that today would be tight for five and comfortable for four.) The henchmen serving would be the sons of other noble families. The tables are covered with large cloths, and there are few dishes or implements on them. The presence of the dog is normal: some Elizabethan tables have an iron loop in a leg to tie a dog to (see figure 1.2). From a French illuminated manuscript, c. 1475. By permission of the British Library.

Furniture as Culture

The furniture that people used can tell us a lot about how they lived. Furniture does not look the way that it does simply because some joiner had a good idea, nor does it change because another, more inspired, joiner had a better one. Equally, furniture does not change or "develop" through a process akin to Darwinian evolution. Darwinian language is widely used in furniture history — it is common

and, up to a point, quite helpful, to say that the joint stool "evolved" into the backstool, or that the sideboard "evolved" from the court cupboard. It only becomes seriously misleading if we unthinkingly adopt the Darwinian assumption that furniture evolution is driven by a natural principle that makes it get better and better all the time: antique furniture forms did not become extinct because they were less well suited to their environment than the forms that superseded them.

The court cupboard is not a dinosaur. Modern furniture is not a higher species than antique furniture. Evolution is a bad model for lovers of antiques.

But furniture does change. This book assumes that we cannot understand that process by the "individual genius" model (by which an inspired maker has the creative imagination to produce a new form), or by the Darwinian "evolutionary" model. The "material culture" model is the one we find the most helpful. This model assumes that the forms of antique furniture are part and parcel of the social order that produced them, and that as the social order changes, so does its furniture, and, of course, all its other arts. The court cupboard took the form that it did because its social order produced a way of living, and therefore of dining, for which it was well suited. The sideboard is the way that it is because it was well suited to an eighteenth-century mode of living and dining.

Georgian society was very different from Elizabethan, but it is misleading to think of it as better. Actually, personally, we far prefer a court cupboard to a sideboard. But that is our taste. We admit that our refectory table is not perfectly suited to a modern dinner party, but our guests enjoy it when we seat them around it, narrow though it is.

Dining Furniture and Cultural Change

Dining furniture provides a particularly good example of how changes in furniture can be most richly understood when we see them as part of much larger changes in society and culture. A cultural transformation lies behind the change from a long, narrow refectory table to an oval gate-leg one. Their solid wooden forms embody different and very abstract concepts of the nature of human beings and of the way that society should be organized. The people who dined at each thought of themselves quite differently; as social beings, which we all are, they differed fundamentally from one another. The social orders of each were organized around quite different principles and values. It may seem a big stretch to think that the dining table we use expresses our idea of our own humanity, and that our idea of our humanity is written into our dining table. But that imaginative stretch is well worth making. If we ask antique furniture the right questions, it can tell us a lot about the lives of the people for whom it was not antique, but new.

LONG NARROW TABLES

The long table, or refectory, table as it is often called today, carries many traces of the society in which it was new. The earliest versions were not even pieces of furniture, as we understand the term today, but were simply boards laid on trestles. A table was not important in medieval and early Elizabethan households. These houses were very sparsely furnished. By far the most expensive and highly regarded furnishings were not pieces of furniture, but textiles — various forms of tapestries, curtains, and carpets (which were not laid on the floor, but on tables, cupboards, and chests). They provided

Figure 1.2: An Elizabethan "withdrawing" table. The massive cup-and-cover legs are united by flat stretchers with the sort of wear that collectors yearn for. On one of the legs is a ring for tying a dog. The bearers supporting the withdrawing leaves can just be seen. When both leaves are drawn out, the top drops down between them to form a level surface. Tongues on the leaves fit into slots on the table ends. Fully extended, the table is 16' long (10' when closed). Courtesy Bob and Sara Hunt Collection.

color, warmth, and a display of wealth. The cloth that covered the table was of greater importance than the table underneath it.

These "tables" were set up for the meal and taken down after it. In Shakespeare's *Romeo and Juliet* (1593) a servant urges, at the end of the meal, "Away with the joint-stools, remove the court-cupboard, look to the plate." His master, Capulet orders, as the dancing begins, "More light, ye knaves, and turn the tables up" (Act I, scene 5). Furniture was moveable, as it had to be, when the same room, in this case the great hall, was used for many different purposes.

During the Elizabethan period, joined tables, which were permanently constructed pieces of furniture, came onto the scene. They were called "dormant," meaning fixed, or not to be disassembled. They were massive, sometimes as long as fifteen or twenty feet, with large, ornately carved legs and aprons. Clearly, Capulet could not have ordered one of these to be turned up. A joined table would have been set on the dais at one end of the hall and would have been used by the master and mistress of the house and their most important guests or family members. Eating a meal was a semi-public event that displayed the social hierar-

ELIZABETHAN HOUSES

From William Harrison, A *Description of England, or a brief rehersall of the nature and qualities of the people of England and such commodities as are to be found in the same.* 1577, 1587.

In plastering likewise of our fairest houses over our heads, we use to laye first a layer or two of white mortar tempered with haire, upon laths, which are nailed one by another, and finallie cover all with the aforesaid plaster, which beside the delectable whitenesse of the stuffe it selfe, is layed on so even and smoothlie, as nothing in my judgement can be done with more exactnesse.

The walls of our houses on the inner sides in like sort be either hanged with tapestrie, arras worke, or painted cloths, wherin either diverse histories, or hearbes, beasts, knots and such like are stained, or else they are seeled with oke of our own, or wainscot brought hither out of the east countries, whereby the rooms are not a little commended, made warme, and much more close than otherwise they would be...

Of old time, our countrie houses, in stead of glasse, did use much lattice, and that made either of wicker, or of fine rifts of oke in checkerwise. I read also that some of the better sort, in and before the times of the Saxons did make panels of horne, in stead of glasse, & fix them in wooden calmes. But as horne in windows is now quite laid downe in everie place, so our lattices are also growne into lesse use, because glasse is come to be so plentifull, and within a verie little so good cheape as the other...onelie the clearest glasse is the most esteemed: for we have diverse sorts, some brought out of Burgundie, some out of Normandie, much out of Flanders, beside that which is made in England, which would be so goode as the best, if we were diligent and carefull to bestow more cost upon it, and yet each one that may will have it for his building...

chy and the differences of rank within it.

At the top of the hierarchy were those seated at the high table — "high" both socially and physically, because the dais lifted it above the other tables. Lower ranks sat at other long tables, which might have been of the boards-on-trestles type, either set along both sides of the hall in a U-shaped arrangement, or along one side in an L. Again, the seating would have been in rank order, the higher ranks being seated closer to the high table. The long, narrow shape of the tables was appropriate to a society that needed to seat diners by rank (a round table does not rank those seated around it in the same way).

Social rank was put on display not only by the seating order, but also by the salt cellar. In the most aristocratic and courtly houses, the master salt was a magnificent and very expensive item, usually made of silver, often gilded and always ornately decorated. With its cover it stood up to 12" high. It was clearly more a symbol than a functional container. Functional trencher salts were filled from the master salt and dispersed along the table. Being seated above or below the salt was a sign of one's prestige. Indeed, the use of the phrase "below the salt" to refer to someone of a lower class lasted three hundred or more years longer than the practice itself. But a person could be seated above or below the salt only at a long table.

Most diners sat with their backs to the wall. Servants served the guests from inside of the U or the L formed by the long tables. But contemporary illustrations do show some diners seated with their backs to the middle of the hall, possibly the lowest-status seats for the lowest rank of diners? We just don't know.

The narrowness of the tables, few of which were more than thirty inches wide, tells us something more about how people lived. Dining was communal, and everything was shared. There were no place settings with a plate, glass, and cutlery for each diner. The host provided the food, the wine, and the serving vessels, but diners brought their own knives and spoons. Cups and drinking glasses were shared, and often spoons were, too. Diners used their fingers to take food from the communal bowl and transfer it to their "trenchers," square slabs of stale bread that, after the meal, were given to the dogs or to beggars. Food and drink were passed up and down the table; no part of a narrow table was out of comfortable reach.

GREAT CHAIRS AND HUMBLE STOOLS

There is an enormous difference between the two basic forms of early seventeenth-century seating furniture – the great chair and the stool. Again,

the difference is social, not wooden. Who sat on what was a matter of extreme importance. At the royal court, etiquette decreed that only the sovereign could sit on a chair; his or her subjects, even the most aristocratic ones, either stood or sat on stools or on cushions on the floor. The great households followed the court: seating was a matter of social hierarchy, not of comfort.

The great chair, often called a "wainscot chair," was throne-like: it was designed to translate social authority into wood. Seated in it at the most important position at the table, the master of the household was literally, as we've called him ever since, the "chairman of the board." The great chair was large and elaborately carved. Its impressive crest and ears were designed to frame and magnify the head of the head of the household. If there were a second chair, it would have been a less elaborate example for the mistress of the house or for an important guest who out-ranked her. If the guest outranked the head of the household, it was the guest who sat in the great chair.

In medieval houses, these "throne-chairs" were massive, canopied pieces that were far too heavy to move. They dominated the hall, and enabled the head of the house to display his rank as he did business, conferred, entertained, or, when a table was set in front of him, dined. In Elizabethan and Jacobean houses, the chair may have declined in size and may have become moveable, even with some difficulty, but it still symbolized social power. In Capulet's house, sig-

Figure 1.3: A great chair and a humble stool. A common arrangement today in which the use of the stool as a table leads us to overlook the social distinction between the two forms of seating. The chair, however, still embodies social power and importance. Its fine crest and ears overlay a halo-like shape upon the rectangular back "to magnify the head of the head of the household." Courtesy Bob and Sara Hunt Collection.

nificantly, the tables, stools, and even the court cupboard were moved aside, but not the chair.

The lower-ranking diners sat on stools or benches. The benches were either built into the walls along the sides of the hall or were freestanding, when they were usually called "forms." Forms appear to have been of lower status even than stools.

Seating by rank was relative, not absolute. In 1503, Henry VII's daughter, Princess Margaret, traveled to Scotland to marry James IV. At their pre-nuptial meeting at the Castle of Newbotell, she sat on a stool and he on the only chair. She showed some discomfort, and, in an act of extreme courtesy, the King overturned the normal rank order: "because the Stole of the Quene was not for hyr Ease [he] ... gaffe hyr the said Chayre."

FLOOR-LEVEL STRETCHERS

All chairs, stools, and tables were made with floor-level stretchers. They provided strength of construction, but they were also a sign of a feature of life that was common to all ranks — a dirty floor. It was strewn with rushes, and while the top layers were changed fairly regularly and sprinkled with sweet smelling herbs and grasses, the bottom ones were another matter altogether.

Early in the sixteenth century, the Dutch scholar Erasmus visited Sir Thomas More, the author of *Utopia*. He tells us that the floor of Sir Thomas's hall was of white clay laid with rushes, and that the rushes in the bottom layer had been there for twenty years! As Erasmus put it, they "harbored in their depths abominations that should have been swallowed by the cess pit." Little wonder that people preferred sitting with their feet on wooden stretchers than on such a floor. There is, incidentally, a gentle irony in the thought of Sir Thomas penning his vision of an ideal society with his feet in a cess pit!

Either Erasmus was exaggerating, or floors improved rapidly, for in 1560, Levinus Lemnus, a Flemish visitor, described the "neat cleanliness" of English houses whose "chambers and parlour strewed over with sweet herbs refreshed me." Paul Hentzner also comments on "the floor, after the English fashion, strewn with hay" (1598).

Only in the richest houses were the floors made of wood. Most were of stone or clay laid directly on the ground. They were thus cold and damp in winter, and rushes or hay served as good insulation for the feet. Many churches had box pews whose sills were deep enough to hold a twelve-inch layer of rushes. The damp floor, incidentally, also rotted the feet of the furniture, so that most pieces have lost an inch or so of height. Oak held up against the damp fairly well, but few walnut pieces have survived with their original feet.

The use of stretchers to raise the sitter a few inches clear of the floor turns out, from today's point of view, to have been a good thing. Seventeenth-century Europeans were small: men were on average five feet tall and weighed about one hundred pounds. Without stretcher–footrests, the tables and chairs that would have been comfortable for them would be low for us.

After the Restoration, the front stretchers of chairs moved to about halfway up the legs, where they could no longer serve as heel-rests. They now could be, and were, decoratively carved or turned. Decorative front stretchers are a sign of clean floors. They also went with a lower table: the gate-leg tables popular at the end of the century were typically two or three inches lower than the long tables that preceded them.

RICH DISPLAY

The court cupboard was the other important piece of dining furniture. To say this is slightly misleading, because its main job was social, not functional. It was there to display its owner's wealth as magnificently as possible,

Figure 1.4: A court cupboard, c. 1590. Now displaying not the wealth of plate but the interest of a collector. The front supports are of the cup-and-cover or melon type, surmounted with Ionic capitals. Here all are carved with the same design, though on many cupboards the upper and lower are carved with different motifs. The rear supports are typical in being unturned, but are decorated, unlike many, which are left plain. The feet are original and rare. Courtesy Private Collection.

which is why so many of them are such impressive pieces. Of course, it also had to act more mundanely as a serving piece, but this function was of no interest to William Harrison, who wrote in his book A *Description of England* in 1577:

Certes in noblemen's houses it is not rare to see abundance of arras, rich hangings of tapestry, silver vessels and so much other plate as may furnish sundry cupboards to the sum oftentimes of a thousand or two thousand pounds at the

The Hall of Jesus College, Cambridge, as it was when one of your authors ate his dinners there in the early 1960s.

DINING (AND LIVING) IN THE HALL

Little changed in the Hall of Jesus College between the seventeenth century and the early 1960s. The master and fellows ate at the high table on the dais, and until 1875, only the master sat on a chair: the fellows sat on forms. In 1875 the main social distinction changed to that between the dons (the master and fellows) and the students: all the dons sat on chairs, while the students continued to sit on forms and on the benches built into the walls, which, incidentally, they reached by stepping nimbly on and over the long tables.

Originally, the hall was one of the buildings of a twelfth-century nunnery that was taken over to form the college in 1496. It was given a new roof of Spanish chestnut about ten years later. Its walls were hung with "arresse" or "cloathes" (probably painted rather than woven to fit the modest economy of a college) that were, from time to time, taken down, cleaned and "ayered abroade." They were replaced by the "Italian" wainscoting in 1703. The floor was stone until it was boarded over in 1875.

Here the main meal of the day was served. For the rest, the scholars ate livery (see p. 80) in their chambers. In 1662, a scholar described his livery in a letter home: "a halfe-pennie loaf and butter or cheese ... a Ciza, that is a Farthing-worth of Small-beer: so that less than a Peny in Beer does serve me a whole day."

In the Elizabethan period the hall was the center of daily life, so the scholars ate at trestle tables that could be taken down after the meal. Then the hall was ready for lectures; for study – it contained "a desk which ye schollers read upon"; and for ablutions – fellows and scholars used the "bason and ewer customably sett upon ye borde over ye stocks" (which were there to discipline unruly scholars!) In winter evenings, scholars pulled their benches around the common fire (now hidden behind the paneling).

The hall was also furnished with a "cort coppord" for the pewter and silver. Everyone ate off pewter, only the salt cellars were silver ~ a clear sign of the symbolic value of salt. The pewter, incidentally, was sent away at regular intervals to be melted down and replaced with new (the estimated life of pewter in daily use was about ten years).

least, whereby the value of this and the rest of their stuff doth grow to be almost inestimable. Likewise in the houses of knights, gentlemen and merchantmen and some other wealthy citizens, it is not geson to behold generally their great provision of tapestry, Turkey work, pewter, brass, fine linen and thereto costly cupboards of plate. ... So in times past the costly furniture stayed there, whereas now it is descended yet lower, even unto the inferior artificers and many farmers, who...have for the most part learned also to garnish their cupboards with plate, their joined beds with tapestry and silk hangings, and their tables with carpets and fine napery, whereby the wealth of our country doth infinitely appear.

This widely quoted extract is worth commenting on. Harrison, we note, is concerned solely with the monetary, and not at all with the decorative, value of the furnishings. It is quite proper that the master of the household should display his wealth openly, and that a guest should be able to assess it accurately. Wealth was a sign of social position. There is also a hint of regret in Harrison's obvious pride in the wealth of England, a regret that the previously visible differences of rank were being blurred by the social diffusion of prosperity.

Plate (i.e., silver vessels) and coins were both made of sterling silver, whose standard was jealously guarded by the Goldsmith's Company. Plate was, quite literally, the savings bank of its day. When the need arose, it could easily be melted down and turned into coins. The need did arise during the Civil War, and the fight against Cromwell was largely funded by the plate of the landed gentry. After the Restoration, the gentry wanted their plate back and kept the silversmiths busy reconverting coins into useful and beautiful objects. This left the country severely short of cash and nearly crippled the economy. In 1696 it was decreed that all silver goods had to be made from silver of a higher standard than sterling. The Britannia standard, as it was called, rescued the national economy.

Ironically, however, the social display of plate was going out of fashion as the solution to the problem it caused was imposed. The move to private dining, which was part of the social changes of the Restoration, reduced the need for the master of the household to put his wealth on display, and so the exhibitionist court cupboard gave way to the functional low dresser.

Public and Private Furniture

The replacement of the court cupboard with the low dresser is a sign of the gradual privatization of domestic life. Furniture that displayed social rank in semi-public settings was obviously ill-suited to a more private lifestyle. The second half of the seventeenth century saw a rapid acceleration of a trend that had begun earlier, the preference for dining privately rather than in semi-public. Elizabethan and Jacobean houses usually contained a "winter parlor" or even one designated as "a ly-

Figure 1.5: Private dining. A set of backstools around an oval table, "convenient for both seeing and conversing." One stool is taller than the rest, presumably for a master of the house who could not entirely forego having his status embodied in in his chair! On the right-hand wall is a newly fashionable low dresser, and on the left, an old-fashioned folding or "credence" table. The portrait is attributed to Mary Beale, one of the many portraitists who flourished in London after the Restoration. Their popularity was a clear sign of the growing importance of the individual in the culture of the period. Courtesy Fiske & Freeman.

tel dyning chamber" off the great hall. These rooms were among the earliest private living spaces, and dining *en famille* was a sign of the growing desire for a private life. After the Restoration, private dining became the norm.

Private dining needed a different table, one that was smaller, less hierarchical, and that was designed to stand alone instead of to fit end-to-end with others. The table made to serve this new purpose was, obviously, of a new shape — circular instead of long. Inventories of the time call these tables "oval" to distinguish them from the "long" tables that they were begin-

ning to supersede; we call them "gate-leg" tables. Their circular form has two implications: it encourages group conversation, and it makes it impossible to seat people in order of rank. Its very form, therefore, is private and familial instead of public and social. It is democratic, not feudal. Incidentally and equivalently, master salts were no longer made in this period, but individual trencher salts still were. The use of these oval tables spread out of the parlor and back into the hall, where, at large banquets, guests were seated in groups around a number of them. In 1679 there were eight tables in the

Great Dining Room at Ham House, and in Badminton House, the seat of the Dukes of Beaufort, there were nine.

In 1669, the Grand Duke of Tuscany, at the end of his travels in England, gave a banquet in honor of King Charles II. The dining was hardly private, but it was, as one might expect, in the new fashion:

> In the middle of the room, the table was set out, being of an oval figure, convenient for both seeing and conversing...Having sat down, his majesty called the Duke of York to set by him on his right hand, and the prince on his left;...[others] to the number of seventeen were accommodated round the table, some on one side and some on the other, and there were as many knives and forks, which, when they had sat down, they found before them, arranged in a fanciful and elegant manner.

Huge though the table might have been, it was convenient for conversation, and was laid with individual place settings (the significance of which will be discussed below). Status was indicated only by the places on either side of the King, not by one's place at table.

No twenty-seater gate-legs have survived: ten-seaters, such as the one owned by the diarist Samuel Pepys (see p. 124), are the largest to be found today. The King's oval table, however, may not have been a gate-leg: Pepys describes another form, "To Sir Philip Warwicke's to dinner, where abundance of company come in unexpectedly, and here I saw one pretty piece of household stuff, as the company increaseth, to put a larger leaf upon an oval table" (May 28, 1665). No oval table of this form has survived. There is, however, a table composed of two semi-circular parts that can be hooked together: this form could have accommodated an inserted leaf (Edwards, 1964: 537).

Around these new tables were new forms of seating: either the caned and carved chairs introduced from the continent, or the native form of the backstool. The former were found in the houses of the nobility and in the town houses of London, where the court influence was strongest; the latter was preferred in the houses of the gentry and yeomanry in the more remote areas, particularly the north of England, where native traditions were stronger than London fashions. What both had in common, however, was the absence of the hierarchical distinction between the great chair and the stool or bench. All the diners sat on similar chairs.

Privacy and the Concept of the Individual

The oval table with its set of chairs, and the long table with its great chair and stools, are documents of quite different types of society. The new social order was moving away from feudalism and toward democracy, and it was beginning to think of its members as people with equal rights, though still of different social standing. The growing desire for privacy is one form of

Figure 1.6: The Great Bed of Ware, c. 1595. Carved and inlaid oak, the headboard with applied caryatids and with painted decoration within the arcades. The free-standing foot posts allow the floor-length drapes to sweep continuously around three sides of the bed. The oak is almost black, the hangings are bright scarlet and yellow, and the headboard is inlaid and painted. The bed gives museum visitors an accurate sense of just how colorful Elizabethan and Jacobean houses were. Elizabethan taste was never muted, whether for carving or for color (see "Bedding the Great Bed," p. 155). By permission of the Victoria and Albert Museum.

this recognition. Privacy became important, because it was privacy that separated the family from the rest of society, and the individual from the rest of the family.

The absence of privacy was a defining feature of a medieval society. Life was social and communal. The manor houses and castles of the nobility and the landed gentry, the farm houses of the yeomanry, and the town houses of the growing class of burghers (urban merchants, artisans, and professionals), were basically built around one room, the hall or great room, to which a service room and a few smaller rooms or chambers were attached. Daily life took place communally, in public, in the hall. Here people ate, slept, did business, entertained, and participated in all the activities of daily life. The medieval house had little private space.

Communal life of this sort involved practices that today, with our strong sense of individual privacy, we would find deeply embarrassing. Medieval paintings and engravings frequently show a couple in bed or even naked in a bath tub surrounded by others going unconcernedly about their daily business. Even beds were not private, but were shared. The Great Bed of Ware, now in the Victoria and Albert Museum, London, was clearly not made for only one couple. On seeing it in 1596, Prince Ludwig of Anhalt-Kohten, was moved to write:

> Four couples might cosily lie side by side,
> And thus without touching each other abide.

The bed, made for Sir Henry Fanshaw in about 1595, was 10' 8" square and 8' 9" high. In 1612 it was bought by the White Hart, a local inn, where its size could be turned into profit: in 1700, for instance, Sir Henry Chauncey records that "six citizens and their wives came from London and slept in it."

An English etiquette book, *Stans Puer in Mensam*, written in the late fifteenth century, shows that social rank was as important in bed as at the table:

> Any tyme that you schall lie with
> Any man that is better than you
> Spyre hym what side of the bedd
> that most best will ples hym, and li
> you on the tother side...Ne go you
> not to bede before thi better cause
> thi [before your better asks you].

In 1530 Erasmus of Rotterdam, the famous Renaissance scholar, published an etiquette book called *De Civilitate Morum Puerilium*. Among his advice on behavior in a shared bed is a piece that modern spouses might well

heed: "If you share a bed with a comrade, lie quietly; do not toss with your body for this ... can inconvenience your companion by pulling away the blankets."

The problem of sleeping with strangers was soon to disappear. Sleeping, like dining, moved from social life into private life. Beds, like tables and chairs, became both less imposing and more numerous. Their symbolic function yielded to practicality and comfort.

Private dining chambers by day often doubled as bed chambers by night. The preference for privacy in both dining and sleeping originated early in the sixteenth century at the top of the social order. The largest Elizabethan houses contained a chamber separate from the hall in which the lord and lady could dine privately: it also often contained their bed. At the public end of the spectrum, too, the shared social values of sleeping and dining shaped domestic architecture and the placement of furniture in a similar way: in the account of the marriage of King James of Scotland to Princess Margaret of England: the wedding banquet was held in the great hall where "ther was also a riche bed of Astat" (1503). A "bed of estate" (or state bed) was one of high social symbolism and was thus appropriately in the same room as a state banquet.

Though privacy increased steadily throughout the seventeenth century, particularly for the upper classes, much of domestic life was still communal. In a communal life, furniture could provide a modicum of personal space and privacy. Coffers and

Figure 1.7: Oak coffer showing owner's initials. Courtesy Fiske & Freeman.

boxes are a case in point. Every one of them had a lock. Some bear the initials or, in rare cases, the names of individuals. Many, of course, would have been used for general household storage, but almost all of the boxes and some of the coffers were used by individuals for their personal belongings. We suspect that the ubiquitous locks were as much to protect privacy as to prevent theft.

An anecdote in the autobiography of Thomas Whythorne, a sixteenth-century itinerant music teacher, allows us a glimpse of how a chest could provide a personal, private space in a crowded household. Thomas traveled with his own chest, and, as was customary, he probably used it to sleep on as well as to store his personal possessions. The mistress of one house was eager to extend their relationship beyond that of teacher and student, so she

> caused a chest of mine to be removed out of the chamber where before that time I was accustomed to lie, and to be brought into a chamber so nigh to her own chamber as she might have come from one to the other when she list without any suspicion. This chamber I was then placed in (Mowl, 1993:170).

Table Manners and the Individual

The increasing popularity of smaller, more private rooms in houses and the development of the furniture appropriate to them is one indication of the steady, if uneven, development of a sense of individuality. In medieval Europe, the individual, in our modern sense, simply did not exist. Modern

English is rich in words for self-identity and introspection that have no equivalent in medieval languages. Today, our assumption that our identity depends upon our individual, inner self is so deep-rooted that it requires hard imaginative work for us to envision ourselves in a society where who we really were would have been determined by our place in the social order, not by any concept of self. Medieval men and women did not think of themselves in the way that we do. The absence of privacy and the absence of individuality are two sides of the same coin.

Perhaps the starkest insight into living in a communal society is provided by its table manners. To us, self-conscious individuals as we are, sharing a cup or a spoon with a stranger would be as awkward as sharing a bed; it shatters our sense of individual differences. But to medieval people, it was normal.

Erasmus's etiquette book (1530) offers us fascinating glimpses into the table manners of a communal society. His advice is directed toward solving the problems caused by a growing sense of individualism in a society that was still deeply communal: it was consistently directed toward minimizing the offense that one individual might cause another as they ate communally. When food is served, "do not poke around in the dish," he wrote, "but take the first piece that presents itself. And just as it shows a want of forebearance to search the whole dish with one's hand, neither is it very polite to turn the whole dish around so that a better piece comes to you."

When fingers served as forks, they obviously became greasy. Diners were admonished always to wash before the meal, and between courses during it. Tables were set with a ewer and basin for pages to pour water, scented with rosemary or chamomile, over the diners' hands. Fingers were to be wiped on the napkin, or even the tablecloth, but should never be licked clean, for that sight was offensive to others. Queen Elizabeth I so disliked greasy fingers that she wore gloves when dining, changing them between courses.

This was not for reasons of hygiene — hygiene is a nineteenth-century concept. It was due to a new awareness that grease passing from one diner to another violated a boundary that was becoming increasingly important: this was the boundary that separated one individual from another. Diners were strictly admonished never to allow their fingers or their lips to touch the rim of a communal glass. "Before drinking, wipe your mouth so that you do not dirty the drink: this act of courtesy should be observed at all times" (Anonymous, 13th century). "Remember to empty and wipe your mouth before drinking" (Erasmus). Even spoons were often shared, and when they were, the same advice applied: "If you are offered something liquid," Erasmus wrote, "taste it and return the spoon, but first wipe it on your serviette." Interestingly, while drink may have been shared, pieces of food should not: "It is not very decorous," Erasmus advised, "to offer something half-eaten to another."

Figure 1.8: Dining in The Netherlands in the fifteenth century. The trestle table is covered with a fine linen cloth and is set with communal vessels. There are five jugs, but only two drinking goblets, three chargers, and three square trenchers of stale bread or treen. Only the salts (six) are the same number as the diners. There is a simple serving table, and a turned stool for the lowliest person. One of the ladies appears to be following Erasmus's injunction not to "poke around in the dish, but take the first piece that presents itself." *The History Bible,* Utrecht, c. 1430. Courtesy Museum Boijmans van Beuningen, Rotterdam.

Another diner's grease on the rim of a shared cup made individuals all too aware of how they differed from others: it violated the sense that each individual was distinct and different. A social order that recognized this difference was obliged to devise behaviors that minimized the offense that one individual might give to others: individuals have a right not to be unnecessarily impinged upon by others. This right, of course, was much less imperative in a communal society

At the end of the seventeenth century, the first sets of tableware appeared, and the problem of greasy lips disappeared. Each diner had an individual set of cutlery, a drinking glass and a plate. The days of sharing a spoon or glass were past, and the abstract concept of the sanctity of the individual was given a material form in silver, in glass, and in the table manners that went with them.

The difference between an oval gate-leg table laid with eight individual place settings in a small parlor, and a long table with one cup and two spoons for eight diners in a great hall, is the same as the difference between Shakespeare's individualized characters and the personifications of vices and virtues that were the characters in the medieval morality plays. In painting, the same development of the individual is clearly marked in the difference between Nicholas Hillyard's portraits of recognizable individuals and the emblematic paintings of saints that were the "portraits" of the Middle Ages. The nature of social identity is a concept of high abstraction: the solid wood of dining furniture is one of its many material forms.

Furniture, literature, and art all reveal the gradual emergence of a sense of the individual out of the communal. This self-determined individual with rights equal to those of others is a fundamentally different being from one whose identity was a product of his social rank and station. During the seventeenth century, people gradually adopted this new sense of who they were: rational, free-thinking individuals. By its end, the English were modern, not medieval. Furniture means so much more when we can see in it the shaping concepts of its social order as well as the shaping hands of its maker.

CHAPTER 2

The Guild System

Joined, Turned, and Boarded

Almost all surviving seventeenth-century oak furniture is joined, that is, it was made by a joiner. Behind that elementary fact lies an elaborate institutional system of guilds and their defining techniques of construction.

Joined furniture was made with mortise-and-tenon joints. In "support" furniture (i.e., seating, tables, and beds), mortise-and-tenoned frames carried the weight. In "storage" furniture (i.e., coffers, cupboards, or chests), the frames enclosed panels floating in grooves in their inside edges. The mortise-and-tenon joint is the defining construction technique of the joiners' guild.

Turned furniture was made by turners on lathes. Joints were made by inserting the end of turned spindles into drilled holes and, often, wedging them tight. Turners made chairs, stools and small livery cupboards, but their main output was utensils for the table and kitchen. The lathe and drill were the tools of the turners' guild.

Boarded furniture was made by nailing or pegging boards together. The earliest stools and benches were boarded, but the most common forms of boarded furniture that have survived today are chests and boxes. Boarded furniture could be made by members of the carpenters' guild, but the joiners' political savvy eventually enabled them to control almost all furniture making, leaving the carpenters to make houses, wagons, coffins and anything else other than furniture.

By the end of the century, the mortise-and-tenon joint lost its supremacy to the dovetail, particularly in case furniture. The dovetail characterized the work of the cabinet-maker and it produced a flat surface suitable for veneering, which replaced carving as the preferred means of decorating wood.

Furniture forms are obviously closely related to woodworking techniques, and one cannot understand one in isolation from the other. Less apparent in the furniture itself, however, is the institution that regulated the craftsmen, their techniques, and their products — less apparent, maybe, but not less important if we are to understand the full nature of seventeenth-century furniture.

The Guild System in Early England

In medieval England, towns grew rapidly as economic hubs for their regions. Though towns were originally market centers, they soon became centers of artisans and craftsmen as well. The quality and prosperity of life within them depended upon civic organizations, particularly the merchants' and craftsmen's guilds, often called "companies." The merchant guilds controlled the selling of goods and produce, whereas the craft guilds oversaw manufacture and production.

Guilds served three main functions:

1. They were fraternal or mutual aid societies: members who had fallen on hard times, through sickness, injury or old age, were cared for by the fit and able.

2. They protected the economic interests of their members. By lobbying national and municipal governments, the guilds were able to restrict trade and manufacture to their own members, to have foreign goods heavily taxed, and to minimize any form of external competition.

3. They protected their customers by enforcing standards of craftsmanship, materials, and fair-dealing.

The huge population of London attracted large numbers of craftsmen with the result that there were enough craftsmen in each trade to form their own guild. In smaller, provincial cities, guilds often encompassed a number of different, but related trades, and their powers of enforcement varied greatly.

Before the tenth century, both the Saxons and Normans had embryonic guild systems that developed into the well-organized and powerful guilds of the Middle Ages. In the early part of the period, many guilds had a formal religious connection that emphasized their mutual aid function. As the Middle Ages progressed, however, the guilds sought their power in corporate and municipal administration rather than the church. In this early period, the merchant guilds were more powerful than the craft guilds, and they became the most influential bodies in early municipalities. In the Elizabethan period, the craft guilds gradually supplanted the merchant guilds in importance. In many English towns today, the Guild Hall is one of the earliest and most impressive buildings.

CRAFT GUILDS

Craft guilds, rather than merchant guilds, are the ones that most interest today's collector. Our antiques were their products, and we can understand our antiques better if we understand how the guilds regulated the craftsmen who made them.

Figure 2.1: The Guildhall, Lavenham, Suffolk. The hall was built in 1529 by the Guild of Corpus Christi, a religious guild that regulated the wool trade. During the reformation, Henry VIII dissolved the Guild because of its Catholicism, and the hall became the (secular) town hall — a good example of how the guild system provided the foundation for municipal governance. By permission of Jim Steinhart of www.PlanetWare.com.

The skills of working in wood, silver, or pewter were deemed a "mystery" or art, and the guilds strove to ensure both that the art was practiced to the highest standard and that it remained exclusive to their members. In 1563 Parliament passed "The Great Statute of Artificers," which decreed that in all trades there should be a seven-year apprenticeship to a master craftsman that had to be completed before the age of 24. The apprentice then underwent a thorough examination by guild officers, and if he passed, became a freeman of the guild. He was then entitled to set up his own business, or to offer himself to a master for employment as a qualified journeyman. Journeymen were paid by the day (from the French *journée*, meaning

day). This hierarchy of master, journeyman, and apprentice was ubiquitous, and nobody outside of it was allowed to practice any craft.

Each guild appointed "viewers and searchers" to inspect members' workshops, materials and products to ensure that there was no backsliding. Because the craft was a mystery, customers could not be expected to have the expertise to check these standards for themselves. The guilds knew that the success of a trade depended at least as much upon trusting and satisfied customers as upon skilled craftsmen. If guilds were to restrict the practice of their craft to their own members, and were to prohibit "strangers and foreigners" from setting up rival businesses, then guild members had to be

TREES AND PEOPLE

The trees growing in medieval England were all hardwoods (the faster-growing, coniferous softwoods were not introduced until the nineteenth century.) Oak was the most widely used wood because of its strength, durability and its reluctance to warp or crack. Elm, walnut, and yew were also used for furniture, as, to a lesser extent, were chestnut, ash, beech and fruitwoods.

England was lightly wooded and densely populated. At the time of the Domesday Book only 15% of the country was woodland. In the early fourteenth century the population was somewhere between 4-1/2 and 6 million and, we may assume, the woodland had decreased. Then came the Black Death, the Hundred Years' War and famine. By 1500 the population had been halved. But in the next two centuries, the period covered by this book, it doubled, and by 1700 had regained its pre-plague level.

This rapid growth of the population, together with its prosperity, created a huge demand for timber. A typical small, two-storey house built in 1600 needed 72 trunks for its framing and studding and another seven for its floor boards. A larger house required more than 330, which was the annual production of 286 acres of woodland (Quiney 1990:48). Incidentally, the transatlantic difference in the naming of floors stems directly from the shortage of timber. The upstairs, which the Americans call the "second" floor was for the English the "first," because it was the first that needed floorboards. The English "ground" floor was appropriately of stone or clay.

These new houses required furnishing rather than fortifying, so joiners added to the demand. Naval commerce was also expanding, and England's enmity with Spain required a fighting navy. The growing iron industry burnt enormous amounts of wood. The native timber simply could not satisfy this demand, so much timber was imported, much was re-used, and joiners and carpenters had to devise techniques that were as economical as possible.

Oak was imported from Denmark. It was called "wainscot" and was of higher quality than English oak, and its straighter grain meant that it could be cut more thinly. It was particularly well-suited for paneling, which was a more economical technique than boarding. The word "wainscot" eventually came to refer to oak paneling, but it originally referred to high quality, imported oak. "Deal" was the word used by English woodworkers for any softwood imported from the Baltic nations. They had never seen the trees that it came from and made no distinction between pine, fir and spruce. Walnut was imported from France and Spain, and from Virginia in the New World.

All timber was re-used wherever possible. The navy had top priority for "new" oak, and many barns and houses were framed and planked with timber whose first use was in a ship. When joiners made mistakes, they used the spoiled piece unobtrusively, where the misplaced holes or mortises would not show. When a piece of furniture was worn out or broken any reusable pieces were reused. Signs of mistakes or of previous use are not in themselves evidence that something is "wrong" with a piece of seventeenth-century furniture.

Figure 2.2: A joined and paneled coffer with panels enclosed by joined frames.
Courtesy Fiske & Freeman.

honest, skillful and, most important, trusted by the public. The viewers and searchers were important officers of any guild. The quality control they exercised was rigorous, at least in the main centers of production.

By the middle of the sixteenth century, guilds controlled almost all the production of goods in what was by now an expanding and prosperous capitalist economy.

FURNITURE GUILDS

Unlike the silversmiths and pewterers, furniture makers were never organized into a single guild. Furniture was produced by differently trained craftsmen. The first guilds to be formed were those of the carpenters and the joiners: the guild of turners came later.

The history of the Guild of Carpenters can be traced back to 1333, at which time it organized all workers in wood. There was then no distinction between builders of houses, farm implements, furniture, coffins and anything else made of timber. The Guild of Joiners was established in 1375 and for the next two or three centuries, disputes between the two companies were frequent, and occasionally, bloody. By the seventeenth century, the Joiners had established themselves as the dominant force in the furniture industry.

JOINERS

In 1440 the Mystery of the Joyners of the City of London was allowed to elect two wardens with powers of search in the city, and in 1613, in London, the Lord Mayor gave to the Company of Joiners the exclusive power of search over makers of cupboards, trunks and boxes, a ruling that began the eventual victory of the joiners over the carpenters. In 1632, the Court of Aldermen, in an attempt to end once and for all the arguments between the two trades, decreed that from that time onwards, only the joiners should be entitled to make:

Imprimis. all sorts of Bedsteads whatsoever (onlie and except boarded bedsteads and nayled together).

Item. All sorts of chayres and stooles which are made with mortesses and tennants.

Item. All tables of wainscotte walnutt or other stuffe glewed with frames mortesses or tennants.

Item. All sorts of formes framed made of boards with the sides pinned or glewed.

Item. All sorts of chests being framed duftalled pynned or glewed.

Item. All sorts of Cabinets or Boxes duftalled pynned glued or joined.

(Glue is mentioned so often because the Carpenters' Guild forbade its use.) The list goes on to include cupboards, wall paneling, doors, church pews and picture frames. It even includes carving (carvers were members of the joiners' guild):

Item. All carved workes either raised or cutt through or sunck in with the Grounde taken out being wrought and cutt with carving Tooles without the use of Plaines.

The victory of the joiners appeared to be complete, except for the making of coffins, which, "... if they bee made of other woode wee conceive fitt that the making thereof be left indifferent either to the Joyner or Carpenters."

CARPENTERS

The carpenters made boarded and nailed furniture such as chests, stools, benches and the boarded beds that were specifically excluded from the joiners' responsibility. Nailing boards together was carpentry, not joinery. They were also allowed to make commercial and kitchen furniture, which they could make more cheaply, if less durably and attractively, than the joiners:

Drapers tables, all tables for Taverners, Victuallers, Chandlers, Compting House Tables and all other tables made of Deale Elme Oake Beeche or other wood nailed together without glue.

They could also make boarded domestic furniture of a lower standard:

... all Sesterne Stooles washing stooles Ducking stooles and all other stooles whatsoever that are to be headed with Oake Elme Beeche or Deale and footed with square or round feete Except all framed stooles glued or pinned.

The "framed stooles glued or pinned" are, of course, what we know as joint stools, but they are all pegged: maybe the glued ones did not survive, or maybe they were pegged later to strengthen them.

In the rest of the country, the two trades coexisted less contentiously than in London. In York, for instance, there was one guild of both joiners and carpenters. In these cases, it was the

Figure 2.3: A side table with drawer, c. 1660. A common form with an uncommon feature: the front and back stretchers are dovetailed, though the side stretchers are mortise-and-tenoned. This is an inappropriate place for the dovetail and required a peg to hold it in place: it is as though a country joiner were trying out this newfangled joint to prove that he could make one. The dovetail was occasionally used on drawers at this time, but did not become common in furniture until the end of the century. In building,

however, it was used much earlier; in 1275, for example, the tie-beams of the barn at Cressing Temple were dovetailed in order to withstand the strong outward pressure upon them. Courtesy Jan and John Maggs Antiques.

apprenticeship system, rather than the guild system, that kept the trades distinct. Apprenticeships maintained this distinction in yet another way: many provincial craftsmen were trained in London because a London qualification was more prestigious than a local one. Indeed, only forty percent of the apprentices registered in London in the seventeenth century became freemen of the company in the city, which suggests that more than half went to the provinces to work. In rural areas where the guilds had no influence, the distinction between the trades disappeared, and the same "artificer" could be both carpenter and joiner: estate records show that oftentimes the estate carpenter made the furniture for the great house.

The Joiners had the political savvy to incorporate potential competitors rather than exclude them: carvers, box-makers and, most importantly, cabinet-makers all became members of the Joiners Company.

TURNERS

Turners and joiners were the most important tradesmen in the production of oak furniture. Their guilds maintained the distinction between the two crafts, but without overt hostility. And at the individual level, joiners and turners worked together harmoniously, often in the same workshops. Almost all seventeenth-century support furniture involved the cooperation of the two mysteries. In 1633, the London Court of Aldermen, recognized that

> the arts of turning and joining are two several and distinct trades and we conceive it very inconvenient that either of these trades should

Figure 2.4: Boarded construction. An end of a boarded coffer with long rebates to take the front and back boards, showing the vertical, cross-grain shrinkage on the horizontal boards. The notches on the edge of the front board are functional as well as decorative -- they help prevent splintering along the grain. Courtesy Fiske & Freeman.

feate and art of turning which they could not do before.

They concluded that "whatsoever is done with the foot as have treddle or wheel for turning of any wood" should be done exclusively by the turners.

The turners were to supply the joiners with any furniture part that required lathe-work — particularly legs — a process that might be seen as the beginning of assembly-line manufacturing. In the early part of the period, the joiners carved the turned legs and posts after they received them, but after about 1640 it became common for the turners to do the decoration on the lathe, and they quickly developed a fashionable repertoire of ball, ring, baluster and spiral forms.

The main products that the turners made on their own were household utensils such as treen bowls, dishes, plates and cups, though they did make some furniture, particularly turned stools and chairs: in about 1620, for instance, the Shuttleworth family of Gawthorpe bought a chair from a turner, whom they called a "dish-thrower"; "throwing" was the same as turning, whether it was pots on a wheel or legs on a lathe.

The turners did not form a guild as early as did the joiners, though their art goes back at least to Roman times. In 1310, the Fellowship of Turners was recognized, but their guild was not chartered until 1604. Even before the 1633 ruling, the Turners had the right to order that all chairs (presumably turned, not joined, chairs) made in London by strangers and foreigners should be brought to Turners Hall to

encroach upon the other, and we find that the Turners have constantly for the most part turned bedposts and the feet (i.e., legs) of joyned stooles for the Joyners and of late some Joyners who never used to turn their own bedposts and stool feet have set on work in their own houses some poor decayed Turners, and from them have learned the

A TURNER'S MURAL CUPBOARD

The construction of this livery cupboard (see p. 80) is typical of the turner: the lathe and drill are the only tools that have been used. The four corner spindles are wedged: these are the structural members that hold the whole piece together. The boards are crudely cut, though they do have a simple molding along the front edge. The molding would have been the work of a friendly joiner as turners were not allowed to own or use molding planes.

The middle shelf is a puzzle. There are unused holes in the top and bottom boards that have no equivalent in the shelf. The crudity of its construction and of the way it is fixed — it does not fit exactly, and it is simply nailed into four of the spindles — suggest a turner's hand that was unskilled beyond the use of a lathe and drill. One possibility is that the shelf was added later, and the spindles on the back of the cupboard were removed to accommodate it. Its front edge, however, is molded identically to the edges of the top and bottom boards. Another possibility is that the shelf is original, but an afterthought: the turner changed his mind while making the cupboard, added  the shelf and never fitted the back holes with spindles. Or possibly he absent-mindedly drilled the holes along the back of the top and bottom boards (they are spaced accordingly), and then corrected his error. In favor of this explanation is the fact that mural cupboards do not normally have spindles along the back — why would they? Also, there are too many holes in each end for them all to have been used at the same time.

Today, everything about the cupboard looks to be of the same age; but then, if the shelf were added only twenty or thirty years later, it would. Interpreting clues is one of the pleasures of living with antiques.

Figure 2.5: A turner's chair. Chairs were the most elaborate objects that turners could make and were consequently showcases of their skill. This is a magnificient example, 56" tall and 27" wide. When we remember that the average man was only 4" taller than the back of the chair, the size is even more impressive. Some of the horizontal spindles are fitted with loose rings that were turned out of the same piece of wood as the spindles themselves, a display of unnecessary but charming virtuosity. Courtesy Fiske & Freeman.

be searched to ensure their quality.

CABINET-MAKERS

The term "cabinet-maker" came into regular use during the reign of Charles II and was another sign of the new taste for luxury. The cabinet-maker took over case furniture, tables, and stands from the joiner, who still made chairs, stools, and beds. The basic difference between them lies in the joints that each used most frequently: the cabinet-maker's signature was dovetailed boards, while the joiner's was the traditional mortise-and-tenon joint. Cabinet-making produced case pieces with flat surfaces that were suitable for the newly fashionable veneering. It was also associated with the change from oak to walnut as the preferred wood of the fashionable classes.

In 1660 there was a small group of specialist cabinet-makers in London. In March 1667, for instance, Samuel Pepys visited "a cabinet-maker, making of a new inlaid table." By 1700 the cabinet-makers had been subsumed into the Joiners, and the Joiners had learned cabinet-making. In that year the Joiners Company claimed that its members were

> bred up in the Art or Mystery of making Cabinets, Scrutoires (desks), Tables, Chests and all other sorts of CABINET-WORK in England, which of late Years they have arrived at so great a perfection as exceeds all Europe.

Any distinction between cabinet-making and joinery rapidly diminished, and the term "cabinet-maker" replaced "joiner" as the regular name for the maker of furniture.

UPHOLDERS (UPHOLSTERERS)

The Upholders' Guild is another that began in the fifteenth century, but it was not until the Restoration of Charles II that it gained social status and power. When Charles returned from his exile on the continent he brought with him a taste for luxury that was new to English society. He appointed Robert Morris to be the King's Upholsterer, and in a mere 21 months, ordered work from him to the tune of £10,000 (our historical currency converter gives that as £8,625,000 or $13,800,000 in today's prices!). From this date on, the upholsterers never looked back, and by the middle of the eighteenth century, they were one of the most powerful bodies in furniture making. *The London Tradesman*, published in 1747, describes the upholsterer as one who

> was originally a species of Taylor, but by degrees has crept over his head, and set up as a Connoisseur over every article that belongs to a House. He employed journeymen in his own proper calling, cabinet-makers, glass-grinders, looking-glass framers, carvers for chairs, testers and posts for beds, ...

Descriptions such as this suggest that the upholders became what today we would call "interior designers."

The upholders had had to fight for their success. In the 1660s, the

Figure 2.6: A dovetailed chest of drawers, c.1680. Dovetails enabled the cabinet-maker to produce the flat surfaces necessary for the now-fashionable veneering and marquetry. All the visible surfaces are veneered, and the marquetry is set into the veneer, not inlaid into the carcass, as it would have been in a joined piece. Courtesy Malcolm Franklin Antiques.

East India Company imported large quantities of rattan cane, and caned chairs became fashionable. They were promoted for their "Durableness, Lightness and Cleanness from Dust, Worms and Moths," and they were cheaper than upholstered chairs. The upholders, supported by the woolen cloth makers, petitioned Parliament to ban the manufacture of cane chairs. They failed, but continued to compete with the chair caners, who allied themselves with the joiners. Much was at stake. In the 1690s London produced about 190,000 chairs upholstered in woolen Turkey work and about 72,000 caned chairs per annum. Between a third and a half of these were exported to the Continent and America.

This enormous production was spurred by the Great Fire of London in 1666 which destroyed 13,000 houses and everything in them. In order to rebuild the greatest city in the world as quickly as possible, the Mayor and Aldermen broke the restrictive power of the guilds, and allowed "strangers and foreigners" to set up businesses. The new fashions for caned chairs and veneered furniture brought to England from the continent by Charles II were satisfied by the continental craftsmen who came to London to help rebuild and refurnish the city.

The weavers were powerful allies for the upholders. Cloth and drapery were costly and of high social status. In sixteenth- and seventeenth-century households, the most expensive furnishings were textiles: hangings for the master bed, tapestries for the walls, cushions and upholstery for chairs and stools, and rugs or cloths to cover tables and court cupboards. The wealth of medieval England, which was considerable, was built largely upon the wool industry. English cloth was widely exported across the continent and across the Atlantic. The spinning and weaving of cloth was a labor-intensive cottage industry in hundreds of English villages and towns from the Middle Ages right up to the Industrial Revolution. It is hardly surprising that the Spinning Jenny and the power loom were the first machines of mass production.

The Decline of the Guilds

The power of the guilds peaked during the Elizabethan and Jacobean periods. The Restoration brought two events that weakened their grip on the furniture industry. The first was the Restoration itself. Craftsmen working for the monarch were not subject to the guilds. So Charles II could satisfy his taste for luxury and continental fashions by bringing into England the "strangers and foreigners" that the guilds prohibited. The second, as we have noted, was the Great Fire of London, which had the same effect: the extent of rebuilding and refurnishing exceeded the scope of English craftsmen, so the City of London had to allow foreigners in, which they did. And once in, the foreign craftsmen stayed. The Joiners' Guild survived through its ability to adapt to social and economic changes. But its exclusiveness

had been broken: it lived on into the eighteenth century because of the benefits it could offer its members, not because of its legally granted powers of regulation and exclusion.

As befitted their medieval origin, the guilds were benevolently autocratic. Their very nature as institutions made them resistant to change, and change was the defining feature of the seventeenth century. Its central decade was the pivot around which fundamental political, economic and thus cultural changes revolved. Many of the traditional characteristics of English life that seemed so securely established before the Cromwellian upheaval lost their pre-eminence after it.

Cromwell did not last long, but he gave an enormous boost to the movement that steadily replaced the power of the monarch with the power of parliament. The huge upsurge of manufacturing and trade after the Restoration accelerated economic trends, such as mercantile capitalism, that were already in motion before it. By the turn of the eighteenth century, London was developing into a center of consumer capitalism, in which being in or out of the latest fashion mattered greatly, and in which fashion changed rapidly (at least in comparison to the seventeenth century, if not to the twenty-first!). A parliamentary democracy based on voting and an economy based upon the consumer are two sides of the same coin: they are also among the most fundamental consequences of the development of the rights of the individual that we traced in the last chapter. The individual, the voter and the consumer all come in the same social package.

The guilds were essentially feudal. In the new economic and political landscape, they simply could not operate as they had in their heyday. They adapted to the new conditions, or they withered away: but they never again shaped the way that furniture was made and thus the way that it looked to the extent that they did in the sixteenth and seventeenth centuries.

CHAPTER 3

Decoration and Style

Stylistically, the seventeenth century falls neatly into two halves separated by the Cromwellian interregnum. Generically, the style of the first half is often called Jacobean, while that of the second is called Restoration. We find the compendium word "Jacobethan" (see Glossary) is useful in referring to the first half of the period, for it helpfully implies that the style runs on a continuum from the Elizabethan to the Jacobean period.

"Elegant by Accident, Magnificent by Design": Elizabethan and Jacobean Style

ENGLISH MANNERISM

The Middle Ages have been called the Golden Age of the English carver. The magnificent churches and monasteries of the period were richly and profusely carved, both their stonework, and their wooden roofs, pews, screens and paneling. The secularization of England that resulted from Henry VIII's break with the Church of Rome diverted this creative energy to domestic, rather than religious, life. After his dissolution of the monasteries during the 1530s, very few churches were built in England for the next 150 years. The carving and decoration that had previously flourished under religious patronage spread to domestic houses and their furnishings. Another factor in the domestication of art was the political stability brought by the Tudors: the great houses no longer had to be strongly fortified, but could be peaceful settings for the domestic arts.

In this newly secular and domestic society, the arts flourished. High artistic quality was achieved by anonymous "artificers" in what we now call, somewhat disparagingly, the "decorative" arts — thus implying their difference from, and inferior quality to, "high" art. High art now resides in art galleries, the decorative arts in museums. The distinction is unfortunate, and the Eliza-

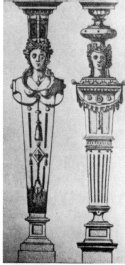

Figure 3.1: Designs for caryatids from Vredeman De Vries, *Pictores, Statuarii Architecti* (1563). No English caryatids looked as silly as the two comic grotesques on the left, nor as fanciful as the two on the right. Craftsmen were more pragmatic than designers and typically toned down their imaginative excesses (this is as true for Chippendale as for De Vries).

bethans were wiser than we in refusing to make it. Their embroiderers, their gold- and silversmiths, their painters, and, of course, their joiners and carvers were the makers of beauty.

Jacobethan furniture is marked by the profusion of its decoration, primarily carving, but also inlay. Today this style is known as "mannerism" — the name derives from *manniera*, the Italian word for manner or style. In mannerism, the manner in which something is depicted becomes more important than the object itself: it is typified by highly developed stylization rather than realistic representation.

Mannerism developed during the later Renaissance in Italy, where it bridged the classicism that preceded it and the extreme ornamentation of the Baroque that was to follow. The primary medium for its northward diffusion was architecture. Architecture was the most prestigious art of its day, and its designs leant themselves well to reproduction by the new medium

of copper-plate engraving. There were numerous design books filled with engravings of architectural details that were ripe for plundering by carvers and plasterers. And plunder them they did. They exploited architectural details with little regard for architectural function: the double volutes of an Ionic capitol, for instance, might be turned upside down and used as a plinth for a figure to stand on, or they might be used within a larger curvilinear design, supporting nothing. The carvers used the principals of symmetry and balance when it suited them, and ignored them when it didn't. Sometimes a motif was repeated on different parts of the piece, but sometimes every motif differs from every other. The motifs derived from classical Greece and Rome, from Turkey and the Orient, from Spain and the Moors, from the Norsemen, and from medieval Europe. The origin mattered not: if it was decorative, it was used.

Few of these designs came directly to England: most journeyed via France, Flanders, and The Netherlands. Generally speaking, the French influence was strongest in the high style pieces made for the court and the wealthiest aristocracy. The Flemish and Dutch influence spread across a broader social spectrum. This may be because the Dutch did not have an aristocracy, so the class of burghers exerted more influence upon art and material culture in the Netherlands than in any other European nation. The English middle classes, who increased in numbers and prosperity from the Elizabethan period onwards, as well as the country gentry and lesser aristocracy, seemed to prefer the taste of the Dutch burgher over that of the French courtier. Furniture made in that style was also, of course, cheaper. There were also close trading links among the English, the Dutch and the Flemish. The last, and maybe the most powerful link of all, was that the Dutch and the English were Protestants in an otherwise Catholic Europe.

Men as well as goods crossed the English Channel in large numbers. Penny Rumble tells us that by 1573 there were over 60,000 Flemish immigrants in England, of whom more than four hundred were master joiners, carvers and turners (1993:23). The English guilds set strict conditions for membership in an attempt to exclude these "strangers and foreigners" (see chapter 2), but the immigrants ignored them and set up their own workshops in such areas of London as Southwark and in East Anglia.

Figure 3.2: A caryatid and atlas, Flemish, c. 1650. The figures support Ionic capitols and taper to plinths decorated with grapes and acanthus leaves. Courtesy Fiske & Freeman.

Mannerist decoration developed into a profusion of abstracted, geometric forms frequently repeated and extended to fill every square inch of the space available. This high decorativism was to be enjoyed for the pleasure it gave to the senses, not for its religious or moral significance, as was the case with medieval art. The promiscuity of decoration that resulted was perfectly in tune with the prosperity and stability of Elizabethan England. The newly secular society sought its pleasures and rewards in the here and now rather than the hereafter. The sensuousness and excessiveness of the Elizabethan aesthetic was thus an early sign of the humanism that was to shape modern Europe. Its detractors

CARYATIDS

Caryatids and Atlantes (the plural of Atlas) are female and male figures used as architectural supports. They are readily found today in a wide variety of forms, so they are eminently collectable. Caryatids (the word is often used generically to include atlantes as well) were developed in the Italian Renaissance from classical models and found their way to England during the reign of Queen Elizabeth I. They survived into the Jacobean period, but are rarely found after about 1640. Cromwell and his puritans must have found the frequently bare-breasted caryatid too risqué and pagan.

The original caryatids were priestesses in Caryae, a town in Laconia, who danced at the festival of Diana. Figures of them were used instead of columns to support the entablature of Greek temples. It is unclear why these particular priestesses should have become architectural supports, but they did. The reason for Atlas becoming their male counterpart is more obvious; he was the Titan who supported the universe and, incidentally, gave his name to the books of maps that regularly used his image as a frontispiece. In Elizabethan English, the verb "to atlas" meant "to support".

In English mannerism caryatids typically take the form of waist-length figures that rest on tapering plinths decorated with mannerist motifs. They support Ionic capitols. The later examples generally retain fainter signs of their architectural origin.

The first pair (left) is Elizabethan, and is typical of the English Renaissance. The realistically carved torsos support Ionic capitals. Below the torsos are carvings of male and female masks in strapwork surrounds whose tapering supports are decorated with further strapwork and guilloches (the carving of the male mask is Egyptian in origin while the lion on the female is classical). The sides are as well carved as the fronts, with satyr masks, strapwork, and guilloches.

CARYATIDS CONTINUED

The other pair (right) is Jacobean.
In them the Italianate influences
of the Renaissance have been
adapted into a northern
European tradition. Both are in
seventeenth century dress. The
carving is more primitive and
"folky" and shows only residual
traces of the architectural roots.

Fragments come with a
double-voiced history. In one
voice they tell the story of
neglect and abuse. Some have
been rescued from houses
and furniture that had been
allowed to decay because they
were deemed old-fashioned
and uninteresting, some of the
earliest came from medieval
churches that were refurbished
in the nineteenth century, and
others, like both these pairs,
from now happily dismantled
Victorian "make-ups" (see p.
179). All of them tell of earlier
periods when the past was not
valued in the way that it is today.

Their other, more positive,
history exemplifies the survival
of the best. History is always
selective, but not randomly: what
we retain from the past always
has qualities that lift it above the
far larger category of what we
discard. In the main, fragments
survived because they were just
too good for people to be able
to toss them into the fire or
the back of the barn. They are
invariably objects with strong
visual appeal and interesting
historical significance.

Figure 3.3: A late Elizabethan coffer, c. 1590. The architectural roots of the design are still apparent: the four caryatids appear to support a pediment that is suggested by the visual separation of the top rail from the stiles. The molded design on the panels echoes that of many Elizabethan gardens (which were also designed by architects.) The deep molding is applied to the flat, sunk panels, and lies below the level of the frame. Edwards illustrates a chest by the same hand, and suggests that the dragons on the rail-pediment indicate a Welsh origin (Edwards, 1964:190-1). Courtesy Fiske & Freeman.

consider its excessiveness to be merely decoration for decoration's sake, charging the carvers with *horror vacui* – the fear of an empty space. But its fans think that its vigorous profusion reflects a vibrant society luxuriating in growth, prosperity and freedom.

English mannerism was the signature style of Jacobethan England. Timothy Mowl encapsulates it beautifully: "...it is a prelapserian world, uninhibited and joyous because nothing is forbidden. The style of Elizabeth and James was only elegant by accident: it was magnificent by design..." (1993:13).

ENGLISH CARVING

The English carvers were closer to folk artists than to the studio painters and architects of Italy. They learned their skills within a vernacular tradition

that was rooted in the medieval gothic and was strong enough to absorb the foreign influence without being overwhelmed by it. This resulted in mannerism with a strongly English accent. To many furniture historians, the mannerism of Jacobethan furniture is the most English of all furniture styles.

The decoration was necessarily shaped by the structural forms of joined furniture. The rails and stiles were carved with bands of running motifs. The panels within them allowed the carver greater scope, and he filled every corner of them with designs ranging from architectural arches, through stylized flowers and foliage, to abstract, geometric patterns. Though there are some straight lines and angular patterns: the overall look of the style is profusely curvilinear. Its curves are of varying radii, sometimes traced by a compass, sometimes free-

A LATE SEVENTEENTH-CENTURY MANNERIST CUPBOARD

This cupboard is interesting as an example of regional anachronism. It was made of oak late in the seventeenth century in rural Yorkshire, where the Elizabethan taste stubbornly survived. Structurally, an Elizabethan cupboard would not have had these long, low proportions, nor the drop finials, and it would not have been fully enclosed. Decoratively, however, the cupboard offers a fine repertoire of Elizabethan mannerist motifs.

These include floral spray inlay in the door panels and houndstooth inlay around them; running guilloches along the top rail; applied caryatid and atlas on the outer stiles, both with Ionic capitols above them. The capitols support a flower that has nothing to do with architecture, but that possibly derives from the roseace. Ionic capitols are also inverted at their feet in a way that is architecturally inappropriate but is quite typical of the way that mannerism adopted a form but discarded its original function.

The central muntin demonstrates conclusively, if we ever had any doubt, that mannerist decoration is not meant to make sense: it is, as Mowl says, "not of the mind, but of the senses" (1993:22). This muntin is decorated with a pile of motifs that bear no rational relationship to one another. Visually, however, they are interesting and attention-grabbing. Reading from the top, they are: an unrecognizable flower, a lion's head, an angel or cherub with crossed wings, an inverted Ionic capitol, and an acanthus leaf. You can either try to make sense of them or you can enjoy them, but you can't do both.

PANELS

Fragments such as these can pack a lot of early England into a small space. They offer the collector the chance to go backward in time: sixteenth-century furniture is rare, but fragments are readily available and affordable, and even earlier ones can be found with some persistence and luck. These panels show the diversity of sources that English carvers drew upon before developing the distinctive style that we now call English mannerism. Hanging them together on a wall is both decorative and historically interesting.

On the left is a pair of "Romayne" panels that is as pure an example of Italian Renaissance style as you will find in English carving. The profiled faces are individualized, recognizable portraits probably of the owner and his wife and the surrounding motifs of birds, foliage and plinths are as Italianate as the name Romayne suggests. This is Italian mannerism before its anglicization.

In the center is an example of gothic tracery whose origins pre-date the Renaissance. Gothic carving derives from the stone masonry of medieval English (and northern European) churches and is of the period when the decorative arts were ecclesiastical, not secular.

On the right above is a Parchemin panel, thought to be a stylized representation of parchment with a fold and curling corners. This example has been so decoratively elaborated that its presumed origin is barely discernible. Linenfold panels such as the one on the right usually retain clearer signs of their presumed origin which lies in the folds of wall hangings. The latter two panels are neither ecclesiastical nor Italianate in origin, but are secular and northern European.

Photos courtesy of Day Antiques, Victor Chinnery, and Fiske & Freeman.

hand, and often, for the tighter curves, determined by the radius of the gouge. This curvilinear exuberance was all fitted into the straight-edged, squared-off shapes of the panels, rails and stiles of joined construction.

Scratch Carving. The simplest decoration was by scratch- and chip-carving. Scratch-carving is not, strictly speaking, carving: the linear designs were merely scratched into the surface with a sharp-pointed tool or a small V-shaped gouge. Scratch carving, like sunk carving (see below), is often combined with punched decoration, usually of small circles. A scratched zig-zag line, for example, may well have a punched circle in each of its angles.

Chip and Gouge Carving. In chip-carving a more elaborate design was scratched onto the surface, often using a compass, and then pieces of it, or chips, were removed with the point of a knife. Typically, three cuts were needed for each of the chips, so that the pattern is composed of an arrangement of shallow, concave pyramids and scratched lines. Closely related to it is gouge-carving, where the chips were removed with one long stroke and one vertical stroke of a U-shaped gouge, giving a more rounded indentation.

Sunk or Flat Carving. The most typical carving of the Jacobethan period is "sunk" or "flat": the background was carved out with a chisel, leaving the design on the flat surface. The sunk background was also flat and was often matted with a punch to contrast

Figure 3.4: Panel in joined frame. The panel carved with foliated scrolls and floral spandrels, the frame with planed channel-and-groove moldings, and chiseled grooves immediately above the panel. Courtesy Fiske & Freeman.

Figure 3.5: Inlaid panel. The inlay of a floral spray and a houndstooth or sawtooth border. Courtesy Fiske & Freeman

with the smoothness of the surface – a contrast that is beautifully heightened by a century or four of waxing. The typical matting punch was about an inch long and half as wide, and carried two rows of five or six pins each.

Relief Carving. Sometimes, particularly with the more realistic depictions of vines and flowers, the surface was not left flat, but was carved to round off the stems, leaves and grapes. This produced a shallow low relief that is considered a mark of quality. A high relief was often employed to depict

Figure 3.6a: Scratch- and gouge-carved lozenge with lunettes.

Figure 3.6b: Flat or sunk carving in the lower band, the initials and date in low relief, the ground matted with a punch.

Figure 3.6c: Arcade enclosing floral design.

human or grotesque figures (known as terms, caryatids or atlantes, see sidebar p.xxx) and sometimes this was deep enough to have been undercut in places, thus becoming partially three-dimensional. Fully three-dimensional figural carving, usually on the supports of court cupboards or on table legs, is comparatively rare and tends to be found on important pieces made earlier in the period.

Carving was expensive, and profuse carving usually indicates a top-of-the-line piece. On more modest pieces, the carving was limited, sometimes to the rails and stiles, sometimes to the panels. Uncarved rails and stiles were usually decorated with channel-and-groove molding produced by a plane, not a chisel.

Inlay. Some pieces, particularly in the earlier part of the period, were decorated with inlay. Black bog oak and the lighter colored holly or sycamore were the inlayer's woods of choice. Holly was often stained green or red to enlarge the palette. On panels, the designs were either architectural, often of arched doorways following the newly discovered principle of perspective, or were floral. On the rails and stiles, inlaid decoration was geometric — typically strips of checkerboard, houndstooth, or rope-twist patterns.

THE VISUAL VOCABULARY OF ENGLISH CARVERS

The decorative luxuriance of Jacobethan carving grew from a surprisingly small number of motifs. But each motif was interpreted differently each time it was used, and it was combined with others in ways that were infinitely new. Jacobethan carving is both utterly conventional and always original: it is always recognizable as Jacobethan, yet every example is fresh and different from every other.

Figure 3.6d: Nulling.

Figure 3.6e: Gadrooning.

The motifs had many origins. The palmette, acanthus, guilloche, lily, and grape-and-vine are found in Assyrian culture from where they spread to Greece some two thousand years before the Renaissance. The Greeks, in their turn, influenced Roman culture, which became the most important single influence upon the European Renaissance. The Romans introduced the taste for such mythological figures and animals as griffins, birds and reptiles; they were also fond of cupids and scrolled foliage. Roman coins were the inspiration for "romayne" panels.

When Rome was sacked by the Goths, the arts migrated to Byzantium, where they influenced Europe again, via the Crusades and also via the Viking invaders and traders. Like the Jacobethan style, Byzantine carving covered the whole area to be decorated, and often included realistic figures in contemporary dress.

Figure 3.6f: Flat-carved foliage of indeterminate form with simplified strapwork on the stile.

Celtic carvers favored interlaced patterns, as well as serpents and dragons, which they drew from Nordic cultures. Arabesque patterns came to Europe via Venice and Spain, which was occupied by the Moors, and in turn, occupied Flanders and the Netherlands, whence the designs spread to England. The Christian church, both Catholic and Orthodox, was yet another source and disseminator. In short, the diffusion of decorative

Figure 3.6g: Quatrefoil motif on a chair back.

Figure 3.6h: Guilloches and lunettes.

Figure 3.6i: Running guilloches.

Figure 3.6j: Arabesque.

motifs across Europe was so complex and comprehensive that precise lines of influence are impossible to trace.

But we can broadly categorize the motifs themselves into four categories: the architectural, the botanical, the geometric, and the figural.

Architectural Motifs. The Norman arch is perhaps the most common architectural motif; it is a semi-circular arch resting upon two plain pillars. English cavers adopted the shape only; they decorated it with floral and geometric motifs that have nothing to do with Norman architecture. Its proportions neatly matched those of the rectangular panel, which is where it is most often found. Such panels are said to be arcaded. Nulling is a series of niches with rounded tops.

Corbels are used to support a ledge on chests or bedheads; the "support" and the ledge are, of course, decorative, not structural.

Botanical Motifs. A popular motif was a flattened open flower usually with three petals and foliage. It is variously identified as a lily, tulip, lotus, or fleur-de-lys. A carving can sometimes be identified as being of a particular flower, but the mannerist stylization has often generalized the motif into a three-petal flower of indeterminate origin. It can even come to resemble the Prince of Wales feathers – a motif that, incidentally, long preceded its adoption by the Prince of Wales.

Then there is a group of stylized flattened multi-leaved motifs that, when roughly semi-circular, are known as palmettes, and when fitted into a more rectangular shape are said to be an acanthus. If they have three or five thinner leaves, they can be an anthemion or honeysuckle.

Another common floral motif is the rose, whose stylized form is known by pundits as the roseace. It is often, accurately, called the Tudor rose and was probably intended to be just that by most English carvers. It is, however, both more widespread and earlier than the Tudors; not every roseace is the Tudor rose, and there is no visual difference between one that is, and another that isn't.

The grape-and-vine was a popular and highly decorative motif that has Christian as well as Syrian, Greek, and Roman origins. It is often carved in low relief, rather than in flat or sunk carving. It may be found on panels, but is more often found running along rails and stiles.

The quatrefoil and trefoil are four and three leaves joined at the centre by their stems. The quatrefoil produces a square pattern that makes it suitable for decorating panels.

Geometric Motifs. Geometric patterns that are laid out with a compass and/ or a ruler are just as ubiquitous as the botanical, and the two are often combined. In their "running" form they are well adapted to the rails and stiles of paneled coffers and doors. In larger sizes they are often found on the fronts of boarded boxes and coffers, and sometimes on panels. Their shapes are often filled with flowers or foliage.

Lunettes are common. A lunette is a semi-circle, usually curving upward like an arch. Running lunettes may be

Figure 3.6k: Romayne panel of a profile in a roundel.

in a simple sequence, or in a double sequence that is interlocked.

Guilloches are circles that are run into each other so that they appear to be two rows of interlinked and continuous S-curves. They are often centered by a rose or other flower. In their running form they are of the same size, but in panels the circles may be of very different diameters.

S-scrolls are what their name suggests. The two curves of the S may be equal or of different radii, and the S may be elongated, sometimes very much so. Often S-scrolls are doubled back to back, or they may be doubled and crossed to form a pair of hearts joined at the point.

The lozenge is a diamond shape, usually filled with other designs.

Gadrooning is a convex fluting usually applied vertically along an edge or rim. The flutes are short with rounded ends, and often taper off at the lower end so that they resemble tear drops. They are usually angled slightly off the vertical and lean away from the center of the design.

Strapwork in its basic form is a pattern of squares, circles and other shapes that appears to have been made by interlaced leather or iron straps often with rivets at their angles. It may be simplified, so that the straps become simple flat lines, or it may be elaborated into ornate patterns in which the arabesque influence is clearly evident.

It appears that boards were sometimes carved with lunettes and guilloches before they were cut to length and used: in many cases the decoration does not fit the length of the rail or stile. This is particularly evident on some coffers where the carving continues from the front rail to the side rail, though interrupted by the upright stiles at the corners.

Figural Motifs. The most common figural carvings are the caryatids applied to the stiles of coffers, bedheads, and wall paneling. Other carvings may support the upper shelves of court cupboards or form the legs of the most elaborate tables. Some are of mythological beasts such as griffins or dragons, but most were human. While these show their classical origins in their form, they were often dressed, charmingly, as Jacobethans. Figural carving is also found in low relief, though rarely. Sixteenth-century panels may contain profile portraits in circular frames surrounded by scrolled or floral decoration; these are typical of the early Renaissance and are known as Romayne. Figural carving reached its peak in the Elizabethan period, and its popularity declined after about 1630.

American Mannerism

English mannerism crossed the Atlantic with the early settlers and became the first decorative style of American furniture. American carving was invariably flat and was combined with applied split spindles and bosses much more frequently than in England. Often the decoration was not carved at all but was painted. Inlay was rarely used. The New England colonists were careful in their selection from the mannerist repertoire. They liked the geometric motifs — lunettes, guilloches, S-scrolls, and nulling — but they luxuriated in the scrolling vines, flowers, and foliage and developed them more richly than did the English

Architectural forms are less common than in England, probably because the arches, pillars and arched doorways were copied from stone buildings: the logs from which American houses were made did not allow for arched forms. Figural carving is notably absent. We may surmise that this is because the figures of English mannerism came from either classical or gothic mythology — and both of these origins would have seemed offensively pagan to the Puritan beliefs of the early colonists. Even Christian images would have been "papist." By contrast, flowers, fruit, and foliage were appropriate motifs for agricultural communities, and their luxuri-

Figure 3.7: Joined chest with two drawers, Hatfield or Hadley, Massachusetts, 1715-1720. Soft maple, chestnut, oak, white pine. The initials HD stand for Hepzibah Dickinson (1696-1761) of Hatfield, who married Jonathan Belding (1694-1778) of Northfield, Massachusetts in 1720. The aesthetic of this chest is established by the paint. The sunk carving is simple and, while matted, serves primarily to delineate the difference between paint colors. Indeed the scratch carving is visually stronger than the sunk. While the motifs of tulips, foliage, and scrolls are common to both English and American decoration, the manner of their carving and painting here is distinctively American. By permission of Historic Deerfield, gift of Dr. Ogden B. Carter, Jr., 96.36. Photo by Amanda Merullo.

A TALE OF TWO BOXES AND ONE MAKER

The fact that the same design appears on two boxes is particularly interesting. First, it illustrates how, in an age without blueprints, a craftsman would repeat a favored design, but never exactly: his memory and hand always ensured differences in execution. More interestingly still, these two boxes show how a design may have crossed the Atlantic.

The upper box, illustrated in Chinnery (1979:333), is painted – the sunk ground in red and the design in blue-grey. The lower box has been refinished but retains a trace of red paint under the lock plate. Chinnery's box is made of oak and pine, the other of oak only. Chinnery's is dated 1691 on the side, the other is inscribed on the side "ME 1689" with a heart carved between the initials and the date. The dates on both boxes are probably later additions.

Chinnery identifies his box as probably American: "The carved tulips are closely related to work from both Essex County, Massachusetts, and the Connecticut River Valley; but it is still not clear whether this is a true American piece, or an English prototype (from Devonshire) from the school of carving associated with William Searle, who was trained at Ottery St. Mary in Devon, and then emigrated to Ipswich in Massachusetts c. 1661. If the latter theory is accepted, then the date of 1691 must be a later addition" (Chinnery, 1979:332).

William Searle was born in 1611 in Ottery St. Mary, where he trained as a joiner. In 1659 he married Grace Cole. The couple is next recorded in Ipswich, Massachusetts, in 1663. He died in 1667. In 1668 his widow married Thomas Dennis, "the best-known American furniture-maker of the seventeenth century" (Forman, 1988:8); Dennis had moved to Ipswich on Searle's death to take over as the local joiner (most towns had only one). He quickly adopted Searle's style, and there is little to distinguish the work of the two craftsmen.

Forman believes that Searle was the craftsman who introduced the florid carving that became so popular New England. He derived it from the floral carving on the medieval pew-ends of his church in Ottery St. Mary (Forman, 1988:136-7). If, as is entirely possible, Searle made one of these two boxes in America (as suggested by the use of pine) and the other in England, the two together provide a remarkably precise example of how seventeenth-century mannerism was carried across the Atlantic. The example is still valid even if the boxes were not carved by Searle himself but by members of the school of which he was the best-known member.

ance might well have symbolized the colonists' belief in the fertility of their new land and their new society.

The Cromwellian Interregnum (1648–1659)

Almost overnight, the social order of England changed from a monarchy to a puritan parliament, and the dominant cultural taste changed in parallel from the ornate to the plain. Very little furniture was made during the Cromwellian Commonwealth and the Civil Wars (1642–1651) that preceded it, but even the disempowered aristocracy had a few pieces made, particularly the newly developed enclosed chest of drawers. Most furniture from this period was made in the plain and sturdy style associated with the parliamentarians. This style had its antecedents in the tastes and furniture of those classes of the yeomanry who considered the court too ostentatious and corrupt, and who feared that it was growing closer to the Catholicism that they hated. They, of course, were the roots of the Cromwellian victory. The difference between ornate and plain furniture expressed simultaneously a class difference, a difference of social morality, and a difference of political allegiance.

The difference was also regional. The strongest royalist support was in the north and west of England, the parliamentarians throve in the southeast and south. These regional political allegiances resulted in the first significant regional differences in English furniture. Before this divisive period, the nationwide influence of the court,

Figure 3.8: A "Cromwellian" chair, c. 1660. A so-called Cromwellian chair of a form that was made in London from about 1630 and that resembles the Elizabethan farthingale chair. It was popular during Cromwell's rule and was exported to, and copied in, America. The shape of the bobbin turnings, the absence of any ring turnings between them, and the proportions of this chair suggest that it was made in England (most American examples have a least one turned ring, often in the center of the front stretcher.) The dry, unpolished surface of the wood that retains traces of its original varnish suggests that it has spent most of its life in America (see "Patina and Preference," p. 185). It may well be one of the original imports. In their period, these chairs were often called "leather chairs," and this one has been reupholstered in old "Russia" leather. Courtesy of a private New England Collection.

Figure 3.9: Applied geometric moldings. On the left, an example from the Elizabethan period; on the right, one from the Restoration. The Elizabethan moldings are applied to the flat panel and are flush with the surface of the frame; their movement is inwards, and they are often called "deep." The Restoration moldings are applied to the surface of the board and lie above it; their movement is outwards, and they are often called "pillow."

and the ubiquity of London-trained apprentices, ensured a national decorative style with only minor local inflections.

It was the ornate, mannerist carving that seemed most offensive to the parliamentarians, so it declined in the areas where their support was strongest. It continued without interruption, however, in the north, and to a lesser extent in the west, until at least the end of the century. Restrained, turned ornaments seemed more acceptable than carving, and so did the applied decoration of moldings, split turnings and blocks that became the dominant style after the Restoration. Turning, rather than carving, provided the decoration of the Commonwealth period.

The two furniture forms that originated in this period — the Crom-

well chair and the enclosed chest of drawers — both conformed to this aesthetic. The chair was upholstered in plain and sturdy leather but enlivened by bobbin or spiral turnings, and the enclosed chest of drawers sported applied, geometric decoration. Surprisingly, perhaps, this geometric austerity was often elaborated by rather fussy bone, ivory and mother-of-pearl inlay.

The Restoration Style

There may have been no hint of classical restraint in English mannerism. But the style that followed was deeply informed by the classical sense of line and proportion. After the Restoration, English tastes changed radically and rapidly. Sinuous curves and profuse decoration gave way to an aesthetic based on straight lines and strict proportions. Geometry replaced exuberance.

In the south, particularly, geometry swept the board. And, once again, it was architecture that carried the taste northwards from its origins in Italy. As Sebastian Serlio put it: "How needeful and necessarie the most secrete Art of Geometrie is for every Artificer and Workeman. Geometrie is the first degree of all good Art." Serlio was an Italian architect of the Palladian school whose works had been published in England before Cromwell's commonwealth. Inigo Jones had built the Banqueting House in Whitehall Palace to Serlian principals as early as 1622, and there are examples of classical geometric design in the Elizabethan and Jacobean period, but the style did not appeal generally to the English taste of the time. This was to change almost overnight: the restoration of the monarchy brought a love of innovation and the desire to leave the past behind. The new style carried no echoes of the mannerism it displaced so completely: indeed, the stylistic change from mannerism to geometry is the starkest in English furniture history.

Geometric decoration was achieved by applying pieces of wood to the surface, thus building it outwards, in contrast to the inward carving of mannerism. Long strips were shaped by a molding plane, cut into short lengths, and then arranged in a variety of patterns. Or the lathe was used instead of the plane, and balusters, bosses, or strings of bobbins were turned, split in half, and applied to the surface. Often slanted and flat blocks of wood were applied to produce an angular "bulge." On top-of-the-line models, these applied pieces were of exotic woods such as snakewood, rosewood, ebony, or cedar, but most often they were of oak. This bulging motif is called "pillow-fronted."

This "applied geometry," as we might call it, is most frequently found on drawer fronts, particularly on the two furniture forms that were invented in this period: the chest of drawers and the low dresser. It was also used on the panels of coffers and on cupboard doors.

(We must note here that a baroque style with a curvilinear exuberance similar to mannerism was fashionable late in the century. Elaborate marquetry-decorated case pieces and side tables, and ornately carved chairs with cane seats and backs, became popular. This taste, however, was largely confined to the court circles and the south. It was characteristic of the Age of Walnut and, with the exception of backstools, had comparatively little influence upon the vernacular oak tradition that is the subject of this book.)

Despite the radical differences between mannerism and geometry, both originated in Renaissance Italy, and both were well suited to decorating joined furniture. The joined furniture of the seventeenth century was English in construction, but Italianate in both of its styles of decoration. By the end of the century, however, the joiner had become as old fashioned as the carver: the age of the cabinet-maker and of veneering had begun.

A VERNACULAR MASTERWORK

This mule chest was made in northern England at the end of the seventeenth century. Its overall aesthetic is clearly English mannerist, but many of its motifs lie outside or on the very fringes of the conventional repertoire. The rather jolly sea-serpents are unusual, though they resemble the dragons sometimes

found on pieces from the west country, Lancashire, and Wales; beribboned lozenges have a long history, but by this date were most popular in Yorkshire and Westmoreland; and the tulip might be found almost anywhere. But the somewhat sinister (or surprised?) masks on the muntins are probably a product of this particular carver's imagination. He, too, may be responsible for translating the conventional, if exotic, trailing grape-and-vine motif into an English pea vine with open pods — if that is what in fact they are.

He has also unified the design. The vertical stiles and muntins carry repeated motifs, and the two horizontal rails echo each other faintly but adequately. He has linked the drawer to the chest by applying the same notched moldings to both, and by repeating the tulip from the muntins. The construction of the drawer-front, incidentally, is interesting: the intricate S-scrolls are carved into the board, but the other decoration is applied in the post-Restoration technique despite the fact that it is carved and not molded.

All in all, this mule chest is a splendid example of vernacular interpretation and originality. It vigorously refutes any disparagement carried by the word "provincial," and contradicts any assumption that the late uses of a stylistic repertoire are necessarily decadent.

A SOPHISTICATED MASTERWORK

This enclosed chest of drawers (c. 1660) dramatically illustrates how completely the Restoration discarded mannerism and replaced it with geometry. It is in two parts. The upper contains two long over two short drawers: the lower has three drawers enclosed by a pair of doors. The architectural influence is seen in the arcaded doorway that follows the newly discovered principle of perspective, the corbels and the dentil molding

around the top, and the pilasters on the front. Not shown here are the sides, which are arcaded with applied rosewood. The decoration is intended to disguise the function — the drawers are barely discernable as such. The doors in the lower part, and the large drawer in the upper are pillow-fronted. Functionally the chest provides ample storage; stylistically, it is an emphatic statement of the new aesthetic.

Its aesthetics are not the only sign that the man who commissioned it was on the cutting edge of his day: his choice of woods was equally trend-setting. The oak and cedar carcass is decorated with applied pieces of snakewood, cedar, juniper, rosewood, ebony and walnut.

Snakewood, sometimes called "speckle-wood" in its period, is a reddish, mottled wood that resembles snake skin. It was grown in Surinam on the Guiana coast of South America. In 1651, Lord Willoughby established a settlement there called "Willoughbyland," which survived until 1667, when the English ceded it to the Dutch in return for New Amsterdam, now known as New York — a good trade on the Englishmen's part, one might think. Willoughbyland sent to England both sugar and snakewood. The cedar in this chest is probably Eastern red cedar from Bermuda or Virginia, and the juniper, a very closely related wood, from there or from the Middle East. Rosewood was imported from Brazil, and ebony from Africa. The walnut may have been native, or may have been imported from the Continent.

The first glimpse of this chest tells us that it was a celebration. It celebrated the return of the monarchy and of a fashionable lifestyle. It also celebrated the global reach of English trade. It exudes confidence in the present and the future, and refuses to look back to the past.

PART II
Forms and Functions

CHAPTER 4
Storage

Boxes

More boxes have survived from the seventeenth century than any other form of furniture, except, perhaps, coffers. Contemporary inventories show that most households owned many of them. Coffers stored larger items, and boxes the smaller ones: almost anything that today we might stuff into a small drawer would have been kept in a box — drawers were rare until the second half of the century. Though the boxes are from the seventeenth century, our common name for them —"bible boxes" — is from the nineteenth. They were obviously used to store far more than just bibles, indeed, boxes outnumbered bibles by many times. We can recall only one record of a bible actually being kept in a box: the inventory of John Coleby, of Amesbury, Massachusetts (1673-1674) included: "Box with linen therein and a bible" (Little, 2001:2).

In 1547, the inventory of King Henry VIII listed many boxes: in the closet next to his privy chamber were boxes containing "painted antiques" (we have to wonder what an antique was in 1547!), "table men" (carved figures, or chess men), "pictures of needlework," "12 pairs of hawks' bells, small and great, and a falconer's glove," "slippers of velvet for women," "burning perfumes," and two or three containing dolls for his children. In 1598, a domestic advice book said that when a lady rides abroad, one of her serving men "is to carrie her boxe with ruffles and other accessories." The household accounts book of the Shuttleworth family of Gawthorpe showed that they bought at least three boxes between 1617 and 1621.

In New England, very similar boxes were used for similar purposes. Nina Fletcher Little tells us that the seventeenth-century probate records of Essex County, Massachusetts, include references to "1 box and some small matters in

Figure 4.1: A typical box. With good flat carving of leafy S-scrolls. Two different punches have been used to decorate the "frame" around the carved area. The initials identifying its owner and the date add to its appeal and value. For reasons that are as yet unclear, dates after 1650 are more frequently found than earlier ones. Courtesy Fiske & Freeman.

Figure 4.2: A homemade box. Not made by a boxmaker. The simplified nulling and the scratch decoration that has been laid out without benefit of compass or ruler lend the box a folky quality. Boxes as amateur as this are often thought to be love tokens, made during long winter evenings by a young man for presentation to his beloved. It's a nice story, and it may even be true. The proportions are unusual. Courtesy Fiske & Freeman.

it, as two small black handkerchiefs, 1 black quoife, 1 bonnet"; "Small squar boxe full of mean books"; "Little boxe with 4 shillings, 2 pence and half a crown" (Little 2001:1).

CONSTRUCTION AND DECORATION

English boxes are typically made of oak, though walnut examples can be found: American ones may be of oak, pine or maple, or of mixed woods, and frequently have pine bottoms and/or lids. Boxes are typically made of boards joined by nails or pegs. Joined or dovetailed boxes are rare. The ends of the boards are often notched to prevent the wood splitting along the grain. The bases often overlap the sides and front, and the lids are hinged by snipe, strap or butterfly hinges. All are fitted with locks; houses in the period were much more public than today's, and personal items had to be kept secure

Figure 4.3: A small box. Nulled and with adorsed (i.e. back to back) C-scrolls. Courtesy Fiske & Freeman.

Figure 4.4: A desk box or "slope." The larger surface and more interesting shape of the end gave the carver more scope than the narrow panel on the front: the carving is more imaginative, deeper, and much more appealing than the conventional design on the front. Courtesy Fiske & Freeman.

and private. Some boxes have sloping lids for writing or reading: these are usually called "desk boxes" in America and "slopes" in England. Many of them have some interior fittings: small drawers, shelves or cubby holes.

The boxmakers' guild was incorporated into the Joyners Company of London. This is somewhat surprising because the boxes were not joined, and the quality of the carpentry is basic. The quality of a box is deter-

mined more by its carving than by any other factor, and the best of the boxmakers were skilled carvers with a vigorous sense of design.

Like most seventeenth-century vernacular furniture, boxes were decorated with repeated, formal patterns that were adapted to fit almost any vertical surface. The decoration is usually flat-carved, though sometimes, particularly with the trailing vine motif, the design is rounded into low relief

Figure 4.5. A desk box with a design similar to one on a paneled chair in Conisborough Church, South Yorkshire. Chinnery illustrates a regular box with this design (1979:366). Fortuitous survivals like these enable us to identify the hand of a particular maker, usually anonymous. The identification is typically of an individual or his shop rather than of a regional style: there are some regional differences in carving but fewer than one might expect. The initials FF, here in an unusually prominent position, are probably the owner's, and were stamped for inventory purposes. They may, however, be the carver's (see p. 97). Unlike carved initials, they add nothing to the value — unless they happen to be yours! Courtesy Bob and Sara Hunt Collection.

— a sign of quality. Lines are usually gouged with a chisel. American boxes are often decorated with applied split-spindles, a decoration rarely found on English ones. Some boxes bear a carved date and/or initials which significantly increases their appeal, and thus their price. The fronts are almost always carved, and sometimes the sides are, too. The backs are always plain, indicating that the boxes were set against the wall, and not, for instance, on center tables.

Most of the dates on boxes come from the second half of the century, after the Restoration. Most post-Restoration boxes are decorated with traditional carving, not with the geometric molding found on contemporary chests of drawers. It appears that the households that equipped themselves with the new-fangled chests of drawers found no use for the old-fashioned boxe; the shallow top drawers now stored what used to be kept in boxes.

And conversely, those that still used coffers for the big items, still needed boxes for the smaller ones. This would imply that the boxes from the Restoration period were provincial.

A box is a great way to dress a larger piece of furniture: indeed, a stack of two or three graduated boxes on a coffer, a chest of drawers, or a side table makes an attractive and striking decorative arrangement. But do fit small felt pads underneath them; their bottoms were nailed on, and sometimes the nail heads protrude enough to scratch the surface they are set on. Boxes are sometimes set on custom-made stands to be used as small tables beside chairs or sofas.

COMMON FAULTS AND RESTORATIONS

Faults that devalue little: Lost lock or hasp, hinges replaced in the eighteenth century, cleats on lid lost or replaced, reinforcing strip inside the lid, small losses or repairs to the wood (especially the corners).

Faults that devalue modestly: newer hinges, repaired hinge breaks (often a new piece of wood at the back of the lid). Faults that devalue significantly: Replaced lid or bottom, later carving.

Coffers (or Chests)

Coffers are as common as boxes. They were the general-purpose storage units of their day, but they were also used for seating and even for sleeping on. All had locks to ensure privacy and security in the crowded households of the period. Some were used for the storage of household goods, but others were personal: most members of the household had their own coffers for their own belongings. Some have initials or names on them to identify their owners.

In the period, the words "coffer" and "chest" described different functions rather than different forms. Coffers were used for traveling or for storing valuables, while chests had a more generic storage function. Most of what we now call "coffers" were, in their day, called "chests."

For the last hundred years or so, however, dealers and collectors have used the name coffer to distinguish these early chests from their eighteenth- and nineteenth-century descendents. The distinction is worth making. In the Jacobethan period, chests were important pieces of furniture that stood in the public areas of the house. Their high status was reflected in the high quality of their decoration and construction. By the eighteenth century, however, the status of chests declined; fewer were made, and those that were were moved from the public to the private areas of the house and from the manor house to the cottage. Their forms subsequently became simpler and humbler. Today, a coffer is, quite simply, a seventeenth-century chest, or, to put it another way, a chest of importance.

CONSTRUCTION AND FORM

Coffers come in two basic forms: boarded and joined. Joined coffers were made by joiners with mortise-and-tenon frames enclosing panels. Boarded coffers were made of boards nailed or pegged together, and could be made by carpenters, or by joiners whose customers were on a budget. Later in the century most coffers had boarded ends: only the front, and sometimes the lid, was paneled. These are known as "joined and boarded."

Smaller boarded coffers are usually made out of six boards, one each for the front, bottom, back, and lid (in which the grain runs horizontally), and another two for the ends (in which the grain runs vertically). The ends are extended downward to form the "boot-jack" feet (the boot-jack shape is made by cutting an inverted "V" into the bottom of the board). The boards are nailed or pegged together, sometimes with simple butt joints, but often without. This can cause shrinkage cracks where the front and back boards are nailed to the ends: the front and back contract horizontally, but the vertical grain at the ends allows for no such

Figures 4.6: A linenfold coffer.
"Linenfold" is one of the earliest conventional motifs in the English carver's repertoire. It was popular from about 1500 and is rarely found after about 1560. This coffer is carved on all four sides, showing that it stood in the middle of the room. The top shows appealing wear from having been used as a seat. The back shows the original loop-and-plate hinges on the rail and loop-and-strap on the lid. Courtesy Fiske & Freeman.

movement. The cleats at each end of the lid can similarly cause the lid to crack. Larger boarded coffers often needed more than one board per surface.

In joined coffers, the panels were set in frames that allowed the wood to move, so they suffer less from shrinkage cracks. The outer stiles extend downward to form the legs. The lids may be paneled or boarded. It is sometimes thought that boarded coffers preceded joined ones and that the joined-and-boarded form was transitional between the two. This is a mis-

understanding: all forms were made over the same period of time, and in fact, many joined-and-boarded coffers post-date many joined coffers. The choice between them was one of cost: joinery was more expensive than carpentry. The most costly coffers, then, were those in which all sides and the lid were paneled.

The other big cost factor was the decoration. In the plainest joined coffers, the only decoration was channel-and-groove molding around the frames. In the most exuberantly decorated, the rails and stiles, together

Figure 4.7 A deep-molded coffer from about 1590. Courtesy Fiske & Freeman.

with the panels they enclose, are all carved. In coffers made before about 1630, carved figures (see "Caryatids," p. 40) were sometimes applied to the stiles. The extent of the carving was determined by the taste and wealth of the owner and today greatly affects the value.

In boarded coffers, any carving is confined to the front, and even this is sometimes only scratch-decorated. Very few are entirely undecorated: a simple groove molding along the front of the lid, a punched pattern, or notched ends on the front board are the least we might expect. The "primitive" simplicity gives boarded coffers a different appeal to the more elaborate, joined examples.

Joined coffers often have a till (a small box) inside for storing smaller items, for coins, or for sweet smelling herbs; boarded coffers rarely do. The hinges may be snipe, strap and loop, or strap. Seventeenth-century coffers were made to stand against the wall, so their backs, whether paneled or boarded, are unfinished. Some sixteenth-century examples were free-standing and were paneled on all four sides; they may have doubled as seats or tables.

Coffers are versatile furniture. They work well under a window, at the end of a bed, or in hallways. Boarded tops make better display surfaces than paneled, which, to our eyes at least, look best on their own. If you intend to store frequently used items in a coffer, get one with a paneled lid, so that you don't have to move your accessories whenever you need to get into it. Smaller coffers are often used as low tables in front of couches to fill the gap caused by the nonexistence of antique coffee tables. People who use them like this do not mind that the unfinished back is visible, although they may choose one with a paneled back.

Figure 4.8: A boarded coffer with home-done scratch carving. Courtesy Fiske & Freeman.

COMMON FAULTS AND RESTORATIONS

Coffers were strongly built and were not moved frequently; consequently many have survived in good condition. Backboards were made of the thinnest wood and have sometimes been replaced; bottom boards may have worn or have been pushed out by heavy contents. Comparatively few original hinges have survived. Boarded lids have sometimes been replaced. The Victorians did not like uncarved oak and "improved" many plain panels and rails with their own version of gothic carving (see chapter 10).

Faults that devalue little: a lost lock or hasp, lost tills or their lids, hinges replaced in the eighteenth century, reinforcements under the lid or to the bottom boards, and small losses or repairs to the wood. Height loss is common, and an inch or two should cause no concern.

Faults that devalue modestly: some replaced bottom or backboards, pieced rear legs (the bottoms of rear legs have frequently rotted for they stood against the wall on the dampest part of the stone floor, newer hinges, replaced rear board of a lid).

Faults that devalue significantly: replaced lid, later carving, major restoration to the wood such as a replaced panel or stile.

Chests of Drawers

While the chest of drawers may be one of the most ubiquitous and useful pieces of furniture, it is also one of the youngest, having emerged only in the second half of the seventeenth century. Chests of drawers replaced coffers and boxes, whose use declined as the chest of drawers gained popularity. Drawers are obviously more convenient than top-opening receptacles. A few early cupboards were fitted with them (now called "enclosed chests of drawers"), and some chests had drawers fitted underneath (often called "mule chests"

Figure 4.9: A joined coffer with paneled lid, c.1630. This coffer has all the features that a connoisseur desires. It is paneled on all four sides and lid, and it retains its original snipe hinges. But what really makes it special is the color of the patination and the carving. The color is dark in the corners and depths of the carving, and ranges to a pale honey where the coffer has received most of the polishing and wear. The carving is profuse, lively and crisply executed. The carver used the techniques of flat or sunk carving, low relief, and gouge-carving. Like many of his colleagues, he covered every square inch of the front, but he had an unusually well-developed ability to unify the different elements into an overall design. Lunettes appear simply on the top rail, and much more intricately in the panels. Similarly, the central columns of the panels and the stiles and bottom rail are gouge-carved in patterns that are different but closely related. The enthusiasm that is usual in English mannerism is here organized into a less frequently found coherence. Courtesy Private Collection.

because they are a hybrid between a chest and a chest of drawers).

The chest of drawers exploded in popularity in the 1670s and 1680s, and many thousands must have been made. The restoration of the monarchy in 1660 had sparked an economic boom and a social taste for ostentation and display. This prosperous and fashionable lifestyle quickly spread from the nobility and the court to the new middle classes of merchants, tradesmen, and professionals. The fashionable clothes of the day were made of

fine materials with delicate decorative flourishes, and they could be stored more safely in drawers than in deep chests.

The new chest of drawers developed in these new middle classes: it was functional and comparatively economical. From here it moved upscale into the houses of the aristocracy, where, by the end of the century, it had become a high-style form, ornately decorated with marquetry. The chest of drawers is, incidentally, the only form of furniture whose evolution was

Figure 4.10: An enclosed chest of drawers, c. 1665, with one of the doors in the lower part opened to show the enclosed drawers, which are always as plain as these. The case, doors and the visible drawers are decorated with moldings, with ebonized split-spindles and bosses, and with applied fretwork that resembles the cut-cardwork of contemporary silversmiths. Courtesy Fiske & Freeman.

upward: most new forms and styles originate at the top of the social order, and then spread downwards in simpler and cheaper forms.

FORM AND CONSTRUCTION

These middle-class chests of drawers were typically made of oak and were always joined: their cases were made of mortise-and-tenon frames enclos- ing panels on the sides and the openings for drawers in the front. The tops were boarded, usually with very thin boards.

Many of the cases were made in two parts, held together by tongues that protruded from the sides of the lower and fitted into corresponding slots in the upper. This is a result of their origin in the middle classes whose houses had steep, narrow stairs that

Figure 4.11: A "mule" chest from Yorkshire, 1700-1720. Raised, or fielded, panels did not become popular till late in the seventeenth century, and in more fashionable areas, they were never carved. Rural craftsmen, however, liked their traditional carving and saw no reason not to apply it to the new fielded panels. Courtesy Fiske & Freeman.

would have been difficult to negotiate with a large case piece. Even chests made in one part were often decorated with a central molding to give the illusion of being in two.

The cases stood either on stile feet — simple and straight continuations of the stiles running from top to bottom of the front and back — or later in the century, on turned, bun feet doweled into the bottom boards. Bun feet are Dutch in origin, while stile feet are an English tradition.

The earliest drawers were heavy and side-hung. Side-hung drawers have grooves cut into each side that run on rails affixed to the sides of the case. This requires the drawer sides to be thick, usually about ¾", and made of a hard wood such as oak. They slide forward easily and don't tip when open, but they are heavy, and by the 1680s, they began to be replaced by lighter drawers that slid on bottom runners. The drawers were usually dovetailed with one or two large, crude dovetails, often reinforced with rosehead nails. Some, however, were butt-jointed and nailed. Their bottoms were nailed on.

Four drawers were usual, though three were not uncommon. The second drawer is typically the deepest; the housewife or maid could store the heaviest clothes without bending! The later fashion for graduated drawers deprived her of this convenience. The top drawer is usually the shallowest. Occasionally, there are two small draw-

**Figure 4.12. A two-part chest of drawers with fine geometric, or "mitered,"
moldings.** Courtesy Private Collection.

ers on the top level, but this arrangement had not yet become common.

The drawer fronts were decorated with moldings applied in a variety of geometric designs. All decoration was pre-shaped with a molding plane or lathe and then applied: there is never any carving. The visual interest of the design and the use of contrasting woods are the main determinants of value.

Joined chests of drawers are still useful in the bedroom but also in the dining room, where their shallow drawers are convenient for cutlery,

and their deeper ones for linens. Do not put too much cutlery in any one drawer: the bottoms were nailed on, and the weight can loosen them.

COMMON FAULTS AND RESTORATIONS

The feet are the main problem. Comparatively few bun feet are original, but many stile feet are. This may be because bun feet were attached to the case by dowels and were thus structurally weaker than stile feet which were integral to the frame. Or it may be because any rotting caused by the damp

THE SURVIVAL FACTOR

This little chest of drawers is made of pine, which today makes it far more uncommon than its oaken cousins. In about 1700, however, when it was made, there were many like it in cottages and farmhouses throughout northern Europe and England. But not today. Oak is hard, pine is soft: their survival rates differ greatly.

The durability of oak can distort our view of sixteenth- and seventeenth-century furnishings. In the wealthy households, walnut was widely used; the homes of the less wealthy contained many pieces made of elm, ash, and other local woods. Damp, woodworm, and neglect have taken their toll on these softer woods, leaving us today a disproportionate amount of oak.

For similar reasons, carved decoration has survived better than painted. Much of the furniture and the interior woodwork of the houses were painted, but very little original paint remains today. Upholstery and fabrics also suffer from low durability. Upholstered stools and chairs were common among the furnishings of the wealthy, but only a small proportion has survived. Dining and side tables, court cupboards, and dressing tables were all covered with table carpets or cloths; the waxed patinated surfaces that attract us today are certainly beautiful but not historically accurate.

The survivability factor can also give the impression that furniture was as important in the period as it is today. This is not the case. Hangings, tapestries, carpets, and needlework, all of which suffer from low survival rates, were the most expensive and most highly treasured furnishings; furniture was more utilitarian.

Durability comes into play in construction as well as material. Boarded stools and benches were less durable than joined: their scarcity is a twenty-first century scarcity, not a seventeenth. We must also factor in social status. Boarded and turned furniture was of a lower status than joined. Being socially disregarded meant that it was readily discarded.

This movement was fueled by enduring utility as much as by quality. As the lifestyles of later generations changed, so did their social requirements, and so did the furniture that met them. If it was old and no longer useful, it was discarded. Similarly, the taste for painted surfaces moved socially downward; painting was cheaper than veneering or polishing, and it disguised cheaper, native woods. Imported mahogany was too expensive and fashionable to be hidden: it needed to be seen for what it was. So carving that had originally been painted was often cleaned and polished to conform to later tastes.

Our tastes are necessarily shaped by what is available to us. But we must not assume that our collections mirror the furnishings of our predecessors. A home furnished with antiques today looks very different from a home furnished with the same pieces when they were new.

Figure 4.13. A side-hung drawer. A detail of the chest on p. 57 showing the side-hung drawer, contrasting woods, and pillow-fronts. Courtesy Fiske & Freeman.

stone floors could not be corrected by cutting off the affected half an inch without impairing their appearance, thus necessitating the replacement of the whole foot. Sometimes stile feet were replaced with bun feet to "improve" the chest. Many chests have been given out-of-period bracket feet: this was frequently done in the eighteenth and nineteenth centuries to make the chests more fashionable.

Faults that devalue little: minor replacements of moldings, replaced rails for the drawers to slide on and a rebuilding of the grooves, slight height loss, or piecing of rear stile feet.

Faults that devalue modestly: replaced rear feet, drawer relinings.

Faults that devalue significantly: replaced top, replaced front feet, bracket base.

Press Cupboards

Most of the cupboards made before the seventeenth century appear to have been made primarily for food. Everything else was stored in coffers and boxes. These early cupboards were called "aumbries" or "almeries." A certain John Smythe listed in his will dated 1543: "A fine almery with fore dores for bread." What is interesting is that the doors were specially noted. Most cupboards were open shelves, or "boards" (see chapter 7). Enclosed cupboards were known as "press" cupboards or sometimes simply as "a press." The Elizabethans were not known for their consistency in language (or in spelling) so we also find in the building contract for Hengrave "... wt ij close pressys, and open pressys round about" (Wolsey and Luff 1969: 40).

Be that as it may, there are two forms of cupboards enclosed by doors that today's collector is likely to be able to find, and afford.

The first looks somewhat like a fully enclosed, and enlarged, court cupboard (see figure 4.14). The display function that was paramount in the earlier, open cupboards had declined by the end of the century. In contemporary inventories, these press cupboards are never listed with a cupboard cloth or carpet, clear evidence that their tops were not used for display. Most were made after about 1630 and continued in popularity until the early eighteenth century, particularly in Wales and the north.

The typical press cupboard was in two parts. Both parts had two doors, the lower ones opening to a shelved interior. The upper part had a panel between its doors and was set back slightly, leaving a ledge about 6" deep in front of it. It had an overhanging top with two turned supports. On

Figures 4.14: Press cupboard dated 1623. The form is entirely typical. The set-back upper portion consists of two doors flanking a central panel. The melon supports, carved with arabesques in a cup-and-cover form, are a hangover from the earlier open-shelved court cupboard of the Elizabethan period (see figures 1.4 and 7.1) where they were structural: here they offer the appearance of support only. The two doors of the lower part are uncarved, and are decorated with channel-and-groove molding. Typically, the amount of carving reduces from the top to the bottom of press cupboards. Courtesy Fiske & Freeman.

Figure 4.15 A standing cupboard from the early seventeenth century. The fine ironwork is original. The feet have been restored, and the top may be a replacement. Courtesy Camcote House Collection.

later versions, these supports shrunk to become drop finials.

The upper, more visible, part was carved, often very profusely, and was sometimes enhanced with inlay. The lower part was sometimes undecorated except for channel-and-groove molding on the stiles and rails, but usually there was some carving, and on some examples the lower part was decorated as profusely as the upper. The top, back, and bottom are boarded, and the whole piece is very heavy. The lavishly decorated cupboards were made for use in the dining room or great hall, the plainer ones for the service areas of the house.

Some press cupboards were built in, and some of the larger ones acted as room dividers in cottages and farmhouses, presumably between the kitchen and the eating area, for they had doors in their backs as well as their fronts.

Press cupboards are currently not popular, and may be bought at reasonable prices, particularly if they are valued at dollars per pound! They are, however, useful both for their enormous storage capacity and for their good display space on top. We are taller than our ancestors. If they have a good color and good carving, they can be very attractive pieces.

Cornices have often been added to conform to a later aesthetic, and the rough boards of the original top have often been

Figure 4.16: A simple standing cupboard whose two flat-paneled doors enclose shelves. The butterfly hinges are original. Courtesy Suffolk House Antiques.

Figure 4.17: A four-door press cupboard, first half of the seventeenth century. Its simplicity suggests that it was made for the service areas of the house, but now its good color, fine proportions and cocks-head hinges would make it welcome in any room. Courtesy Suffolk House Antiques.

replaced with smooth finished ones to provide a better display surface. Neither of these modifications have much effect upon the value in today's market (provided that the cornice is small and unobtrusive). Many press cupboards have been reduced in size, and the collector should generally leave these alone as they are of decorative value only.

These press cupboards were impressive pieces of furniture, but there were other enclosed cupboards that were more utilitarian. These smaller, one-piece cupboards tend to date from the first half of the century or earlier: in

Figure 4.18: A clothes press from the early eighteenth century. The fielded panels and their shaping at the top of the doors have "modernized" a late seventeenth century form. The row of panels in the base have "honestly" replaced the more usual false drawers, behind which is a continuation of the hanging space. Courtesy Suffolk House Antiques.

the second half, the larger cupboards in two parts were more popular.

As befits their utilitarian purpose, these smaller cupboards were rarely carved: their doors were either boarded, or flat paneled, though some later examples had geometric moldings applied to them. The decoration is usually confined to channel-and-groove molding on the rails and stiles, or sometimes on the boarded doors themselves. The pierced openings in food cupboards were usually decorated.

A clothes press was a two-part cupboard whose upper part was an open space enclosed by two doors and whose lower part contained drawers. A few had a pair of doors in the lower section as well. The upper part was for hanging clothes, and many retain their original pegs. If there were two or more rows of drawers in the lower part, the top row was often a false front behind which was a space to accommodate the longer clothes hanging from above.

These clothes presses still serve their original purpose well. Some have been fitted later with shelves to serve as bookcases, but they are too shallow to be adapted into entertainment centers. You may sometimes see them called, confusingly and wrongly, livery cupboards, presumably because they could have been used for servants' "livery" (their uniforms, that is, not their rations — see below). Clothes presses are good looking but not in fashion. If you need an attractive cupboard in the hall for your outdoor coats, you should be able to buy one comparatively cheaply.

Food Storage

ARKS

Arks were small chests used to store grain, flour or meal. Most were made between 1500 and 1650. They had canted lids that were often reversible

for use as kneading troughs. As utilitarian pieces, arks were rarely decorated, and they were not subject to the changes of fashion, so they can be hard to date with any precision. Most of the arks that come on the market today were made in the sixteenth century. In their period they were known as "arks" in the northern counties (where Arkwright is still a common family name), and as "hutches" in the south and west of England. Today, we usually call them arks regardless of their origin, because the word "hutch" can refer to other forms of furniture.

Visually arks are rather boring, and they are of limited use in today's home, though they can make good log boxes beside a big, open hearth. For collectors, however, they are fascinating. Arks are one of the few pieces of Tudor furniture that today's collector has a realistic chance of acquiring at a realistic price. For someone interested in the history of methods of construction, arks are particularly appealing because they were made by the clamped-front method, which is the earliest form of joinery.

The clamped-front first appeared as early the thirteenth century and was used only to make chests and arks. In a clamped-front chest, the horizontal boards of the front are slotted into deep grooves in the inside edges of the stiles. They are secured by oak pins, and thus the whole front is "clamped" together. The grooves are often 2" deep or more. Sometimes the board ends are cut into tongues to slot into the groove more easily.

Before the clamped-front method was developed, chests were

Figure 4.19: An ark made in Wales between 1550 and 1625. It is 36" wide, 20-1/2" deep, and 25-1/2" high. It clearly shows the clamped-front method of construction in which the front boards are slotted into deep grooves in the stiles. Interestingly, it also uses an early, almost embryonic form of a pegged mortise and tenon joint: the canted boards of the lid are tenoned through the side rails and held with a single peg. The lid pivots on oak pins that extend from the top back board through holes in the rails of the lid. There are no nails or ironwork anywhere in the piece. The three-board, canted lid is typical, as is the way that the sides narrow slightly towards the top. Unusually, this ark is decorated with scratch carving on the front and lid. Courtesy Fiske & Freeman.

either hollowed out from a log or were boarded. Clamped-front chests are less laborious and wasteful than hollowed ones, and stronger than boarded ones. The clamped-front is the predecessor of the mortise-and-tenon, a joint that first appeared in the second half of the fifteenth century and allowed the construction of joined and paneled chests, a lighter and more elegant form. By about 1600, joined chests had replaced clamped-front ones in all but the most rural areas.

Arks were often made with no ironwork. All the joints were secured by wooden pegs, and the lids were either loose or were pivoted on wooden pins that extended from the backboards and went through holes in the side rails of the lids.

Livery Cupboards

Before the Restoration, households ate one large meal a day in the middle of the afternoon. At other times, people ate "livery," that is, food that did not need cooking and that could be given out (*livrée*) to each member of the household. The other meaning of the word — a servant's uniform — derives from this one; retainers eligible for livery wore livery. These personal rations were stored in livery cupboards. *The Liber Niger*, published in 1483, tells us that each member of the household was given "for his Livery at night, half a chet loaf, one quart of wine, one gallon of ale, and for winter livery, from All-Hallowtide till Easter, one percher wax, one candle wax." A candle was typically part of a livery. By today's standards, the food and drink, particularly a quart of wine and a gallon of ale, would seem more than adequate for a good night's sleep! Livery was eaten late at night and early in the morning, and so, as contemporary inventories confirm, livery cupboards were often part of the furnishings of the bedchamber.

In his list of "Things usefull about a Bed, and a bed-chamber" Randle Holme includes

> an Arke or safe: a kind of little house made of wood, and covered with haire cloth, and so by two rings hung in the middle of a Rome, thereby to secure all things put therein from the cruelty of devouring Rats, mice, Weesels and suche kind of Vermine. Some have the pannells of the Arke made all of Tyn, with small holes for aire, others of woode.

The larger food cupboards, or aumbreys, were made in the fifteenth and sixteenth centuries. As late as 1573 Thomas Tusser, in his *Five Hundred Points of Good Husbandry*, still used the term:

> Some slovens from sleeping no sooner be up,
> But hand is in aumbrie, and nose is in cup.

We cannot tell if Tusser here was referring to an outdated form or was using an old word for what we know as a livery cupboard.

Most livery cupboards were mural, but a few were made to stand on the floor, and some examples, very rare now, were hung on ropes from the ceiling (Holme suggests that this was once the normal form). Mural livery cupboards were small, just large enough to hold one or two liveries. All were ventilated. Hanging them kept the livery out of the reach of the ubiquitous rats and mice, and, we assume, from the cats and dogs that preyed on them. Many were beautifully decorated with carving, inlay, and applied ornaments, often with a strong architectural influence. Some, however, were "turner's cupboards," made entirely of spindles inserted into holes in the boarded tops and bottoms (see p. 31). These cupboards were among the larger items that turners were able to make: consequently they can rival turner's chairs as showpieces of turnery (see figures 2.5 and 5.23).

One type of food cupboard was used for charitable not domestic purposes. Now sometimes called "dole cupboards," they were placed in churches and in gatehouses for the scraps left from a meal to be given to

Figure 4.20: A sixteenth-century aumbrey (or standing livery cupboard). The name "aumbrey" derives from the French *almerie*, which has the same root as "alms," the term for food given to the poor. It is thus an appropriate name for a food cupboard. In its period, however, an aumbrey, or "almery," was for general storage, not just food: Henry VII's queen, Elizabeth of York, for example, had an aumbrey "for to put in the bokes." The typically shaped ventilations on this example clearly indicate that it was used for food. Today, the name aumbrey is often used for any cupboard of an early seventeenth- or sixteenth-century date. Courtesy Camcote House Collection.

Figure 4.21: A mural livery cupboard, c.1620. The high quality of this cupboard suggests that it was made for the lord's bed chamber, where it would have been admired by the important guests received there, as well as by the lord and lady themselves. It carries an example of almost every decorative technique of its time – turned spindles, applied split-balusters, applied caryatids or terms, inlay, flat or sunk carving, pierced fretwork, and architectural corbels. Courtesy Private Collection.

the poor or to passing travelers. This custom of giving alms was a social obligation for the wealthy, and most great houses were like Marchalsea in having "a littell olde almery in the logge at the gate" (1483). Henry VIII decreed that, at his Eltham Palace, "All the relics and fragments be gathered by the officers of the Almery, and be given to the poore people at the utter gate by oversight of the almoner."

Large households would have needed numerous livery cupboards, but comparatively few have survived. In the second half of the seventeenth century the practice of eating one large meal supplemented by livery died out, livery cupboards became redundant, and succeeding generations saw little point in keeping them. Today, however, their small size, decorative appearance, and rarity ensure that they fetch high prices when they do come on the market.

There is also a distinct form of standing livery cupboard that resem-

Figure 4.22: An unusual food cupboard. It is floor-standing, so it was probably used for dole rather than livery. It is made like a coffer, but its lid has never been hinged, and its back is of short, vertical boards, so it was not a conversion from one. Courtesy Fiske & Freeman.

bles a court cupboard with an enclosed upper shelf. They were used for the distribution of livery and not for its overnight storage, so we treat them as serving pieces in chapter 7.

SPICE CUPBOARDS OR BOXES

Spice cupboards may have hung on the wall or stood on a side table or court cupboard. People took their food very seriously in the seventeenth century — their recipes were elaborate and delicious. Every house had an herb garden, but native herbs were not enough for the gourmands of the time: they wanted tastes that only imported spices could provide. Spices were highly regarded and expensive. Consequently, spice cupboards are both beautiful and lockable.

They all take the same form: an arrangement of small drawers, usually nine or twelve, enclosed by a door with a lock. Today, they serve well as jewelry cabinets in the bedroom or as organizers in the home office. Less functionally, their beauty and small size make

them fine decorative accessories anywhere in the house.

GLASS CUPBOARDS

Though they were not for storing food, glass cupboards are appropriately dealt with in this section because of their resemblance to mural livery cupboards. Drinking glasses were expensive, beautiful, and hard to replace when broken. Their fragility required safe storage: their expense and beauty, public display. The shelves of glass cupboards often had decorative lips to ensure the safety of their contents, but were open and unencumbered by spindles or pierced-work. The glasses were easily visible, easily accessible, and safe. Glass cupboards do not have doors. In some the shelves are large enough to suggest that they contained delftware as well as glasses. In inventories they are listed with names such as "glasse cupberd," "glasse shelves," or, charmingly, "glase peartch." They occur most frequently in the inventories of yeomen's houses, which can lead us to infer that drinking glasses were among the yeoman's most treasured possessions, and so deserved special display and storage. In wealthier households, perhaps, they may not have been quite as prestigious.

Glass cupboards are the small forebears of the delft rack. Delft racks replaced them in the eighteenth century when pottery and glass became more widely available, and thus less special. Delft racks were found in kitchens, where their display was certainly decorative, but was not intended for public admiration.

Like livery cupboards, glass cupboards are small, beautiful and rare, and thus comparatively expensive. They can be highly decorated or very simple, a range that reflects the room in which they were hung, or the social class of the household.

A Caveat to Close With

Wolsey and Luff warn us that we may be too precise in assigning specific uses to mural cupboards: any of them may have been used for any small objects such as salt cellars, spice containers, or oil pitchers, as well as glasses and livery (1969: 42-3). In particular, they note that they have never seen stains on a livery cupboard that would provide conclusive evidence that it did in fact store bread, cheese and beer. Randle Holme says that the hanging cupboards that he calls "arks" were used for "all things" that needed to be kept out of the reach of vermin, presumably more than just food. Matching the terms used in contemporary

Figure 4.23: Spice box, c.1700. The arrangement of the drawers is unusual and attractive. The large lower drawer is dovetailed, so that it is strong enough for contents heavier than dried spice. All the pulls are original: those on the smallest drawers differ because, we may assume, the other pattern was not available in a small enough size. Note the gouges on the inside of the door to accommodate the pulls when closed. Courtesy Private Collection.

inventories with surviving pieces of furniture is an interpretive art, not a precise science.

Figure 4.24: Boarded and carved glass cupboard, c. 1635. A larger-than-usual glass cupboard with profuse carving and architectural features. Most glass cupboards are carved and are of nailed, not joined, construction, which suggests that they may have been made by boxmakers rather than joiners. Courtesy Private Collection.

But, whatever its original use, today a mural cupboard helps solve the problem of what to hang on the walls of a room furnished in early oak. It also makes a distinctively decorative feature in a more eclectically furnished room: we have one among the modern cabinets in our kitchen.

CHAPTER 5

Seating

Joint Stools

Joint stools were made in large quantities in the sixteenth and seventeenth centuries. They were the most common form of seating but also served as small tables and as footstools. There were, for instance, 170 in Lord Lumley's estate when he died in 1590. Many stools were made in sets, sometimes matching the long table around which they were used. Joint stools were socially ubiquitous: they were used in the homes of yeoman farmers and town burghers as well as in the most aristocratic houses.

English inventories give us glimpses of how numerous joint stools were:

"The joined table and half a dozen joined stools belonging to it." (1585)
"Great joined table, 6 joined stools and one walnut-tree chair." (1586)
"Great Chamber, one drawinge table of walnutte cutt and carved of three leaves long, and xii stooles cutte and carved." (1594)
"In the parlor, One long table, eighteene joined stools, two chairs." (1681)

In America, Richard Lumpkyn, of Ipswich, Massachusetts, had "one table with six ioyned stooles" (1642).

Randle Holme (1649) illustrated a typical example, and described it as "a Joynt stoole ... so called because it is all made and finished by the Joyner, having a wood couer." He distinguished it from a turned stool, "made by the turner or wheelwright ... wrought with knops and rings" (see figure 1.8). Joined stools were also distinguished from boarded stools, which were nailed and made by carpenters. No seventeenth-century turned stools and very few boarded stools

Figure 5.1: Joint stool with turned and carved legs. The legs are a reduced version of the cup-and-cover legs on Elizabethan long tables and court cupboards. These place it early in the period, 1600-1625. Carving on turned legs declines in popularity after about 1625. Courtesy Private Collection.

have survived. There were also upholstered stools made for the wealthiest households: early examples are hard to find, but ones from the William and Mary period are occasionally available. But for today's collector, the stool of choice is the joint stool.

FORM AND CONSTRUCTION

The variations among joint stools, particularly in height, suggest their various uses. Stools of 20-22" high were used for sitting at table: their height enabled the sitter to rest his or her feet on the table stretchers, thus keeping them off the dirty and draughty floor. (Tables of the period were 32-34" high, compared to the 28" height of eighteenth-century ones, and the 30" height of nineteenth-century and modern ones.) Stools 18" high were used for seating in other places, or in

workrooms such as the kitchen: people sitting on them rested their feet on the floor. There are also stools of 12-16" height that were foot stools or children's stools. At the other end of the scale are a few stools taller than 22": these were probably what were sometimes referred to at the time as "stoole tables." These (much less common) stools often have thinner legs and occasionally a larger overhang of the top, indicating that their main use was as small, easily moveable tables. The legs of the taller stools were splayed at the narrow ends for stability, but on footstools (or children's stools) they were usually straight.

Other variations include stools with hinged tops over a small storage compartment, and a few with a drawer fitted under the seat. Both these forms are rare and cost two or three times as much as a regular stool.

Figure 5.2: Joint stool with simple barrel-and-ring turned legs and a light, airy appearance. These features place it later in the period, 1650–1675. Courtesy Fiske & Freeman.

Figure 5.3: Joint stool with vase-and-ring turned legs. The seat rail has a shaped lower section that cants outwards, a feature that is found on many stools made between 1600 and 1640. Courtesy Fiske & Freeman.

The frame of a joint stool consists of four turned legs joined at the top by seat rails (also called an "apron" or "frieze") and, just above floor level, by stretchers. The legs and rails may be carved, the rails and stretchers may be molded. Before about 1640, it was quite common for the lower edge of the seat rail to be scalloped. All the joints are pegged mortise-and-tenons. The top had ovolo molded edges and was pegged to the frame in one of three patterns: one peg into the top of each leg, or one into the middle of each rail, or two into each long rail and one into each short. Tops have often been nailed to the frame later for extra security and have often been replaced.

Joint stools are occasionally called "coffin stools." Predictably, the Victorians are responsible for this misnomer, which may well trace back to an entry in Pepys's *Diary* (published in 1825): "...my uncle's corpse in a coffin standing upon two joint stools..." (6 July 1661). Note, however, that Pepys calls them "joint" stools. While joint stools are undeniably versatile, their primary function was to support the living, not the dead.

Because joint stools were common and of low status, later generations discarded them without thinking, or relegated them to cottages and barns where they deteriorated rapidly. Almost no sets and very few pairs have survived. Their survival rate was low, but today their versatility and small size means that the survivors are eagerly sought after; as a result they are comparatively expensive (backstools generally cost less than joint stools, for example). A joint stool beside your chair is the only form of antique furniture that puts your wine glass at exactly the handiest height.

CLOSE STOOLS

A close stool is much the same height as a joint stool, and today serves equally well as a small table beside an armchair, though it has the added advantage of storage. Most have had their interior fittings removed, and sometimes their carrying handles. In their day, close stools were also known as "necessarie stooles" or, more attractively, "stooles of ease."

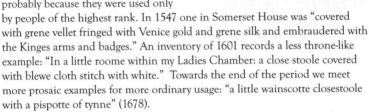

Early examples were richly covered, probably because they were used only by people of the highest rank. In 1547 one in Somerset House was "covered with grene vellet fringed with Venice gold and grene silk and embraudered with the Kinges arms and badges." An inventory of 1601 records a less throne-like example: "In a little roome within my Ladies Chamber: a close stoole covered with blewe cloth stitch with white." Towards the end of the period we meet more prosaic examples for more ordinary usage: "a little wainscotte closestoole with a pispotte of tynne" (1678).

Most of the examples on the market today are of this later form, and most disguise their function by pretending to be something else, usually a miniature chest of drawers ~ a disguise that makes them readily acceptable in today's living rooms.

Close stools can be distinguished from the much rarer box stools by the depth of the lid which is about two inches deep to accommodate the padding on the seat inside (a "stoole of ease" really was an appropriate name.) Their social change from being richly decorated symbols of rank to more modestly functional objects is perfectly in synch with the general changes in lifestyle and taste discussed in chapter 1.

COMMON FAULTS AND RESTORATIONS

Detecting a replaced top on a joint stool can be tricky. A piece of old oak can easily be cut to size and pegged correctly: because stools did not vary much in size, a top from one may well fit the frame of another. To be certain make sure that everything is right – the color-match and shadowing underneath, the pegging and later nailing (if present) on top: wear on the edge molding, and shrinkage cracks, or a gap if the top is of two boards, provide welcome confirmation.

Faults that devalue little: minor height loss, minor repairs to the top or feet.

Faults that devalue modestly: replaced stretcher or rail, all feet replaced.

Faults that devalue significantly: replaced top (often a top from another stool), two or more replaced stretchers or rails, replaced leg, later carving.

Figure 5.4: Two box stools. The one on the left with the more usual lift top, that on the right with a less common fall front. Courtesy Bob and Sara Hunt Collection.

Wainscot or Joined Chairs

When the Duke of Tuscany visited the Earl of Pembroke in 1669, his secretary recorded that

> there was prepared for his highness, at the head of the table, an arm-chair which he insisted upon the young lady's taking; upon which the Earl instantly drew forward another similar one, on which the serene prince sat, in the highest place, all the rest sitting on stools. His highness obliged the earl to take the place nearest to him, though in his own house; and there were at the table, besides all his highness's gentlemen, the sheriff and several other gentlemen, in all sixteen. The dinner was superb, and served in a noble style; they remained at the table about two hours.

This account is typical of the seventeenth century: its focus is not upon the furniture, but upon its social use. What mattered most to the actors in this mini-drama, and to Magliotti who recorded it, was the enactment of social authority, both in deciding who sat on a chair and who on a stool, and also in who had the power to make that decision. In this case, the guest outranked the host, and was thus the decision-maker. Magliotti described the process of getting seated in detail: the dinner itself he covered in a sentence.

The magnificence of the chair in comparison to the simplicity of the stool was a social requirement. It came, not so much from the owner's sense of his own importance, but rather from the need to give the social hierarchy a material presence. People were comfortable knowing where they sat. The grandeur of the chair was underscored, we need to remind ourselves, by the fact that the man sitting in it would have

Figure 5.5: Boxed chair (c. 1685). From Derbyshire or Yorkshire, where the Pennine winters are cold and windy. The boxed base served both as storage, reached by lifting the hinged seat, and as a draught-excluder that extended up to the panels under the arms. The decoration is confined to the deep molding on the stiles and rails, and to the shaping of the crest rail. A good example of plain and sturdy furniture with all the no-nonsense character of the community where it was born. Courtesy Suffolk House Antiques.

been, on average, only five feet tall, and one hundred pounds in weight.

In its day, the wainscot chair was often called, simply, a "chair"— a chair had arms, and the name was enough to distinguish it from a stool or a backstool. Sometimes it was called a joined chair to distinguish it from one made by a turner (see below), and sometimes, as in the account above, an armchair. But whatever we call it today, wainscot, joined, paneled, or arm, the seventeenth-century chair is the one form of furniture that was not disregarded and discarded in subsequent periods. Today it is perhaps the most eagerly collected of all forms. Wainscot chairs are beautiful, widely varied in decoration, deeply characteristic of their period, and, when fitted with a cushion, surprisingly comfortable. It is no wonder that they have remained a treasured part of English domestic life over the centuries.

CONSTRUCTION

The joined chair derives from the fixed throne chairs of the Middle Ages. In its earliest form it was, as Randle Holme puts it, "so weighty that it cannot be moved from place to place, but still abideth in its own station." These early sixteenth-century chairs were typically boxed in to the ground with a seat that lifted for access. Their backs were paneled, and on the sides the panels reached from the ground up to the arms. The panels were carved with linenfold or Romayne work, and the overall appearance was thoroughly medieval. By Elizabeth's reign, chairs had become lighter and more mobile, and

Figure 5.6: Wainscot chair. With the barrel turnings typical of the mid-seventeenth century. The arcaded panel shows the close design-relationship between the panels on chairs and coffers. The molding that frames the panel on this chair back is more finely detailed than we would expect to see on a coffer because it is closer to eye-level, and is on a higher-status piece of furniture. Courtesy Suffolk House Antiques.

the paneling was often confined to the back alone.

The backs of joined chairs vary widely, both in construction and decoration. Until about 1630 the top rail of the back was usually set between the upright stile, but from about 1600 onward, we begin to find top rails set over the stiles, sometimes protruding a couple of inches on either side with scrolled ears between their underside and the outside edge of the stiles. The

Figure 5.7: A plain and sturdy chair. With a simple lozenge and square, chamfered legs. Courtesy Jan and John Maggs Antiques.

backs may have one or two panels, they may be fitted with crest rails, even the top rails that are tenoned into the stiles may have additional crest rails above them. In some later examples, the panels may not extend down to the seat.

The carving may, in rare and expensive examples, be figural, but most is of mannerist, floral, geometric, or running designs. It may cover the whole back — panel, stiles, rails, and crest — or it may be limited to a few, or even one, of these elements. In earlier chairs, the backs may be inlaid, either with mannerist floral sprays, or with more austere geometrically interlaced "knots." The quality, extent, and rarity of the decoration is critical in determining the value of the chair.

Sixteenth-century chairs had horizontal arms made from horizontal boards that scrolled outward. By the seventeenth century, the arms began to be set higher in the back so that they curved downward toward the front. They were now made of vertical boards. These sloping arms were open and rarely paneled in as many of the horizontal ones were.

After the Restoration, the wainscot chair went out of fashion in the south, but it flourished in the north where it became, if anything, even more elaborate and magnificent. These profusely carved northern chairs typically have large, double-scrolled crests with scrolled ears beneath them. They were clearly designed to magnify the head of the head of the household (see figure 1:3).

The English wainscot chair is a magnificent sign of status and still exudes grandeur and authority. The comfort that it offers, however, differs from that of a modern chair. Neither wainscot chairs nor the wing chairs that developed from them were designed for the post-nineteenth century fashion for lounging or for constantly changing position when seated. They were designed to be comfortable in one position only, one of dignit: our grandmothers ("sit still, sit up straight") and our chiropractors would thoroughly approve. At the end of the century, in the fashionable south at least, comfort superseded status, and the fully upholstered, and in its day very expensive, wing chair was born. Padded upholstery replaced carved panels. But comfort was achieved at the expense of magnificence: uphol-

Figure 5.8 **Wainscot chair, Yorkshire, 1650-1700.** The most decorative elements are the crest and the ears, which remained visible while the chair was in use and were therefore what mattered most to the man of the house. The carving of the lozenge is conventional, that of the crest and ears is more imaginative. Courtesy Fiske & Freeman.

Figure 5.9: An upholstered wing chair, walnut, c.1710. This chair has the "new" cabriole legs of the Queen Anne period, but retains the tall hump of William and Mary chairs and settees. Courtesy Private Collection.

stered wing chairs lack the grandeur of the great wainscot chair that preceded them.

AMERICAN JOINED CHAIRS

In America, wainscot chairs are rare. Probably, their grandeur and their hierarchical role made them ill-suited to the avowedly egalitarian culture of New England. But whatever the reason, few were made and only about 200 have survived, of which most were from the mid-Atlantic: fewer than 20 were from New England (Forman 1988:145-46). Most have much less carving than their English counterparts, and their arms tend to be more horizontal.

There is a group of six, made in Essex County, Massachusetts, probably by the same hand. Distinctively American, they have become known as The

Great Chairs. They have horizontal arms and square-sectioned balusters for the front legs and arm supports. Their backs are composed of two horizontal panels, and the carving is confined to the top panel and its frame.

Another, very different, chair is from Ipswich, Massachusetts. Its carving equals English examples in its profusion and quality, and it is thought to have been made by William Searle between 1663 and 1667, not many years after he stepped off the boat from England. It, too, has horizontal arms. Wainscot-type chairs were more popular in Pennsylvania, and many more have survived. Most are of walnut, whereas the New England chairs are all oak.

Backstools

The joined backstool is the first "dining chair," as we would call the form today, within the oak tradition. The change toward private dining in small groups around an oval gate-leg table, which occurred in the second half of the seventeenth century, brought with it the need for a new form of chair to replace the wainscot chairs and joint stools of the first half of the century. Both the new table and its chairs minimized the differences of social rank.

In London, and in the aristocratic houses where the influence of the court was at its strongest, these new chairs followed the continental fashion (see figure 5.11). They were typically made in walnut, elaborately carved, with high, caned backs and caned seats. As we noted in chapter 2, they were made in huge numbers

Figure 5.10: Backstool with a paneled back and well-carved crest rail. Courtesy Fiske & Freeman.

Figure 5.11: Walnut caned chair. The crown celebrating the restoration of the monarchy was a widely used motif. The scrolled front legs are continental in origin, and are unlike anything in the English tradition. Courtesy Fiske & Freeman.

and widely exported. Bowett (2002:89-90) finds in them traces of mass production and the division of labor. He considers that on these chairs, at least, the small stamped initials that are usually understood to be owners' inventory marks, are, in fact, journeymen's marks. Caned chairs required the work of carvers, turners, caners, and joiners, and the stamps identified the work of each. Bowett goes on to argue that this suggests that the journeymen were paid by piece-work rather by day-rates (as their name would otherwise imply). This division of labor shows that manufacture and assembly were quite separate operations, and may not all have been carried out in the same shop. Chair caners appear to have been a distinct group within the joiners' guild, and may well have worked in separate premises. The principles of mass-manufacture long pre-date Henry Ford.

"THE CURIOUS AND INGENIOUS ART AND MYSTERY OF JAPANING"

Japanned armchair, beech, c.1690.
Courtesy Fiske & Freeman.

In the last quarter of the seventeenth century, lacquered furniture imported from China and Japan became all the rage. In 1688 Stalker and Parker published a widely popular book *Treatise of Japanning and Varnishing* to help English craftsmen counter the imports brought in by the East India Company. The Joiners' Company twice petitioned parliament to ban the trade in order to save "the Art of Cabinett Making [from] ruine and distruction." Unfortunately, many politicians owned shares in the East India Company, so the petitions fell on deaf ears.

Japanning is the name given to English attempts to imitate oriental lacquer. Three or more coats of colored varnish (black, green or red) were laid down for the background; the design was then raised with coats of a gesso-like paste, then colored, and finished with more coats of varnish.

The japanning on this armchair is simple, but charming: it has a folk art quality because it was almost certainly done by an amateur. Japanning was a fashionable accomplishment for ladies, and, perhaps even more important, improved the marriageability of their daughters. Edmund Verney clearly recognized this when he wrote to his daughter in 1689:

"I find you have a desire to learn Jappan, as you call it, and I approve of it; and so I shall of anything that is Good and Virtuous, therefore learn in God's name all the Good Things, & I will willingly be at the Charge so farr as I am able – tho' they come from Japan & from never so farr & Looke of an Indian Hue and Odour, for I admire all accomplishments that will render you considerable and lovely in the sight of God and man."

"THE CURIOUS AND INGENIOUS ART AND MYSTERY OF JAPANING" CONTINUED

The fashion lasted well into the eighteenth century. In 1729 Mrs. Delaney wrote to a friend, "Everybody is mad about japan work; I hope to be a dab at it by the time I see you."

Stalker and Parker scorned "those whiffling, impotent fellows, who pretend to teach young Ladies that Art, in which they themselves have need to be instructed" (Bowett, 2002:161).

This chair was made to be japanned: it is made of beech, not the better-looking walnut, and it has a number of surfaces that have been left plain and waiting for decoration. The most obvious are the central splat, the circles under the crowns, and the blocks at the top of the front legs and of the stiles on the back. Figure 5.11 shows a virtually identical (walnut) chair on which all these surfaces are carved.

These elaborate chairs and the efficiency of their production were typical of London. The provinces, particularly in the north, were more traditional. In them, traditional craftsmen met the tastes of an increasingly prosperous class of yeoman farmers, landed gentry, and merchants who followed English traditions rather than London fashions. They, too, preferred dining in intimate groups: they, too, adopted the oval gate-leg table, but around it they placed sturdy, native backstools.

As its name implies, the backstool derives from the traditional joint stool, to which a back was added for comfort. The name distinguishes it from the wainscot chairs of the native tradition, and from the caned chairs of fashionable society.

Backstools are recorded as early as the fifteenth century, but they were not common. In Elizabethan and Jacobean England there were some chairs with backs and no arms, usually upholstered in "turkey-work" or leather, that we know as "farthingale chairs," and during the Cromwellian Protectorate, a form of backstool with a low square back, also upholstered in leather, became popular, particularly in the south of England; it is known today as a "Cromwellian chair." But it was not until after the Restoration that backstools were made in quantity. Both the caned chair and the Cromwellian chair were made in America, particularly in Boston, but the joined backstool remains a uniquely English form.

FORM, CONSTRUCTION, AND DECORATION

Joined backstools had plank seats, some with lips to help hold a squab cushion, and a wide variety of backs. Their legs and stretchers vary little: they are block-and-turned, with blocks at every join, enabling the joiner to use a strong mortise-and-tenon joint. Between the blocks are turnings in any combination of balls, rings, balusters, and spirals. The side stretchers are

Figure 5.12: Cromwellian backstool with the newly fashionable spiral or twist turning and leather upholstery. During the Commonwealth some backstools were wider and lower than the form that became traditional, giving them a more horizontal look (see also figure 3.8). Early spiral turnings were carved and rasped by hand, but soon a lathe was developed that moved the workpiece sideways against the stationary chisel. Courtesy Fiske & Freeman.

man best exercised his imagination and skill, and where today's collectors look to exercise their choice. The usual back is about 40" high. It earliest form was a solid panel with a crest rail, both carved, that derived directly from the back of the wainscot chair. Later versions had thinner, vertical panels between stiles, or four vertical molded splats, or vase-shaped splats. Some had elaborately carved horizontal rails, often in the shape of an inverted crescent — the variety is almost endless.

The tall or high backstool is a less common form that was a rural version of the fashionable caned chairs of London. It echoed their high backs (about 46-48" high) and vertical proportions, but the caning in the back was replaced with a tall, narrow panel set between turned stiles, or with vertical splats, and its seat was boarded instead of caned (caning was a newfangled skill confined to London artisans.) Like its prototype, it had an arched, ornately carved or pierced crest rail. Often the carving on the front stretcher echoed that of the crest rail or the side splats. Tall backstools are slightly more expensive than their more traditional cousins.

Backstools were made singly and in sets, though few sets have survived, and even pairs can be hard to find. You can capitalize on their huge variety of backs by assembling a "harlequin" set. A harlequin set is an interesting combination of unity and variety: the unity is provided by the basic form and by a set of squab cushions to make the chairs more comfortable, and the variety by the differently carved and shaped backs. A harlequin set is more

usually square sectioned, the front is usually block-and-turned. Most backstools have two side stretchers to take the stress of someone leaning against the tall back. The backstools made before Cromwell were fairly high, and the front stretcher was low enough to serve as a footrest. After the Restoration the seats were lowered to a modern dining height of 17" or 18", and the front stretcher generally moved to half-way up the legs.

The back is the most important element: this was where the crafts-

Figure 5.13: Typical backstool backs and crest rails.

Figure 5.14: A selection of typical backstools from the late seventeenth century.

interesting visually than a perfect set, and can be more interesting to collect. An oval gate-leg table surrounded by backstools is both attractive and useful, either in a traditional kitchen or in a country dining room.

COMMON FAULTS AND RESTORATIONS

Backstools were the first chairs with backs that had no arms to help take the strain when the sitter leaned back. Joints have often broken out and been repaired or have needed tightening, some have blacksmith's iron reinforcing brackets underneath. Their feet have often been ended out. Most repairs are obvious, though a well replaced seat may be hard to detect.

Faults that devalue little: tipped legs, especially the rear, minor joint repairs, reinforcements under the seat.

Faults that devalue modestly: a replaced stretcher, a replaced board in the seat.

Faults that devalue significantly: replacement of the seat or of any important element, later carving, a chair made up of parts from two others.

Benches or Forms

Joynt Forme, or Bench. These are termed Joynt formes, because wholly and workmanlike made by Artist of the Joyners craft. Some are made with turned feete, 4 or 6 according to its length, haveing railes or Barres both above for the seat to be

A FARMHOUSE WINGED ARMCHAIR

This generous, characterful chair was made of oak at the end of the seventeenth century in the north of England. It is a local version of the caned walnut armchairs that were fashionable in the south. It has splats instead of caning on the back, and the seat is boarded. It has lost some height through wear.

The side wings are its most unusual and interesting feature. They are never found on the fashionable prototypes, though they appear quite frequently on country chairs (see figures 5.23 and 2.5). The farmer would have draped a cloth around them and drawn the chair up to a blazing fire. The fire would have toasted his front, and the cloth would have kept the drafts from his back. The more brightly the fire roared, the more heat it gave, and the colder the drafts it sucked in under the door and around the windows. He needed the cloth around the back of his chair.

But nobody has recorded what sort of cloth it was. Did the farmer throw his heavy cloak around the back? Had his wife stitched flour sacks together to hang on it? Had she treated him to a length of homespun, or even of woven material bought on one of their rare trips to Halifax or York? Had she sewn loops or pockets to fit over the finials? We just don't know.

The humble history of everyday folk is never written in archived records. Antiques are the documents of humble history. But the stories they tell are full of gaps, and the gaps are a source of pleasure, for they stimulate our imaginations to fill them.

---

fixed upon, and below, to hold the feete firme and stiddy.

So Randle Holme describes benches or forms (the two terms were used interchangeably, though "form" was the more common in the period).

Many great rooms or halls had benches built into the walls; moveable ones were used on the room side of the tables. Contemporary inventories also show that forms were sometimes placed at the ends of beds, where they were used for conversation.

From the thirteenth to the sixteenth centuries forms were made by carpenters and were "nailed and boarded" — the seats were supported on a shaped board at each end. From the Elizabethan period onward, how-

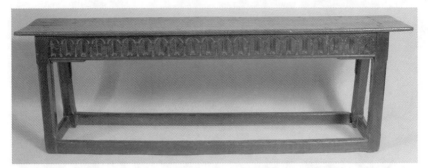

Figure 5.15. An early seventeenth century form. At 63", it is longer than most. It has square chamfered legs, and the nulling is on one side only, presumably the side facing into the hall. It may also have been used in the servants' quarters. Courtesy Fiske & Freeman.

ever, joined forms with legs became standard. In construction and decoration, forms are like elongated joint stools. But they are far less common, and they lost favor steadily through the seventeenth century. Inventories cited by Chinnery (1979:263-4) show, however, that forms were still in use in the seventeenth century even though they were rarely made: "In the Hall... one table bord, one forme, 5 stolles..." (1615): "In the hall...One long table, eight joyne stooles, two joyne formes" (1686).

In seventeenth-century America, forms were used in private houses and public buildings: in both they were of low status. Forman tells us that "by the third quarter of that century, [forms] were not sufficiently individualized to remain acceptable in the public room of a New England house. In 1677, for example, a form was used in the kitchen of William Hollingsworth's house in Salem, while chairs graced his 'best roome'" (1988:145).

Forman goes on to argue that as the humblest form of seating, benches were typically used by women and children. He refers to an engraving (figure 5.16) that shows a mother and children sitting on a bench listening to their husband-father who is, as befits his patriarchal authority, sitting in a chair. Their public use was similar: "Forms were also used for group seating by the less affluent in many New England meetinghouses and courthouses" (Forman 1988:145). Wolsey and Luff agree on the low status of forms: they suggest that in England they were used mainly by servants (1969:68).

Their low status, combined with their lack of utility in later households, meant that forms were discarded without much thought. Today, few have survived, but the ones that have are certainly not low in favor: they are two or three times as long as a joint stool, but may be three or four times its price. Collectors like them because, apart from their rarity, they are one of the very few forms of unmodified antique furniture that can serve as a coffee table, although a narrow one, in front of a sofa. We could also consider putting one, as the original owner might have, at the foot of the bed.

Figure 5.16: Seating by rank. The man is sitting on a turned chair with a thick cushion. His wife and children appear to be seated on a form. Notice the lattice-work window and the mannerist decorations framing the picture. Woodcut in *The Whole Psalmes in Foure Partes*, London, 1563. Courtesy Jesus College, Oxford.

Settles

Settles are benches with backs and arms that seat two, three, or four people. They were often set next to the hearth, and so the backs of most reach to the floor to prevent draughts from swirling around the feet of the people toasting in the warmth of the fire. Most have arms at both ends, but some have a solid arm-rest at one end only: this indicates that they were set at right-angles to the hearth, with the solid arm toward the room.

Most settles were multi-purpose pieces that were used for storage and for sleeping as well as sitting. Their seats are often hinged lids that lift to storage boxes. In 1600 the Petrie family of Ingatestone, Essex, owned, "a bench settle with two chests and two lydds,

having two locks and two keys." A few have a row of drawers under the seat, and some, made in the eighteenth century, have a tall, shallow cupboard built into their backs, usually accessed from the rear. They are known as "bacon settles" because bacon was hung in them to cure. Today, the hooks usefully take outdoor clothing.

One of the earliest recorded references to a settle is the "langsedile" (Latin for "long seat") in Durham Abbey in 1454 (the term "longsettle" still survives in the north of England). Darwinian historians of furniture argue about whether the settle evolved from a coffer fitted with back and arms, or whether it descended from a wainscot chair stretched sideways. The date of this reference seems to suggest that it began as an independent piece

Figure 5.17: A large paneled settle from the last quarter of the seventeenth century. Its vertical, (i.e. not canted) back clearly shows, even at this late date, its derivation from the settles that were built-in to the wainscoted walls of the hall. Courtesy John Andrews.

Figure 5.18: A settle with an early form of raised panels on the back and three molded drawers. The finials and turnings on the legs suggest an origin in Cheshire, c. 1690. Courtesy Fiske & Freeman.

Figure 5.19: Settle/table, Welsh, late seventeenth century. A dual purpose piece that was made for a Welsh farmhouse where the kitchen was the main living area. "Many settles, particularly in the smaller homes of south-west Wales, had backs which swung forward to form a table." (Bebb 1994:8-9) Making efficient use of limited space was typical of Welsh furniture, as were the shoe feet. For use as a table, the top slides in the grooves in the arms so that it can be centered over the base. Courtesy Fiske & Freeman.

of furniture alongside both coffers and chairs, but its later history clearly relates it to chairs, even though coffers were used as seating.

Whatever its origin, a settle is an evocative piece of furniture. It is closely associated with the warmth of the hearth, with shared, communal convenience, and with the heart of the seventeenth-century rural home. It is, of course, much older than that, but

sixteenth-century examples are to all intents and purposes unobtainable to today's collectors.

The earliest settles were simply crude benches built in to the walls of medieval houses. Sitters rested their backs on the wall paneling. The first moveable examples simply attached the paneling to the seats rather than the walls: the seats and their bracket supports are heavy and primitive look-

Figure 5.20: A country pub settle with a planked back and lollipop finials. The table folds up against the back when not in use to make an (uncomfortable) third seat. Its massive construction of dense, native oak, the rectangular-sectioned legs, and the dual-purpose design suggest that it was made in south Wales (where it was found). Its construction and design are seventeenth century, but in rural areas both continued well into the eighteenth. Courtesy Bob and Sara Hunt Collection.

ing, but their backs are of fine paneling, usually linenfold.

Most of the early oak settles on the market today were made in the second half of the seventeenth century in the north of England, where the winter nights were longer and colder than in the south. These cosy pieces of furniture continued to be made for taverns and farmhouses throughout the eighteenth century and well into the nineteenth. The simple, draught-excluding form changed little over the centuries, but only the earlier examples were carved and decorated. Later settles had plain, planked backs, and were usually made of deal. The early settles that interest us here were made of oak, their backs were more often paneled than planked, and they were carved, often all over, but sometimes only on the crest rails and stiles. The carving is similar to that found on the wainscot chairs of the region, which means that it can be very enthusiastic on northern examples.

Early American settles are rare, and, as with most American country furniture, are not carved. Their backs are usually paneled, and they some-

Figure 5.21: A settle from late in the seventeenth century with a profusely carved back. The overhanging crest rail and ears are typical of armchairs. Courtesy John Andrews.

times have storage under the seats. They were made in both New England and Pennsylvania, with the New England ones usually being of pine, and the Pennsylvanian of walnut. Wallace Nutting, opinionated as ever, thought that when a settle was placed in front of a fire, "it obviously spoiled the unity or attractiveness of a room" (1921:311), but Benno Forman, more constructively, argues that where the front door opened directly into the main living room, as in many southeastern Pennsylvanian houses, a settle could have formed a small entrance lobby that deflected the draught from the center of the room (1988:189).

Today settles are often used in hallways, where they are useful both to change shoes and as places to set the grocery bags as they are ferried from car to kitchen. This location often leads to them being wrongly called "hall benches." Benches do not have backs. The Victorians were responsible for moving settles from the living and working areas of the house to the entrance hall, and from country farms and inns to suburban homes. They made many "Jacobean" settles for this new use, all of which are ornately carved, meanly proportioned, and ugly.

Turner's Chairs

Randle Holme described turned stools and chairs: "A Turned stoole...This is termed because it is made by the Turner, or wheele wright all of Turned wood, wrought with Knops, and rings all over the feete, these and the chairs

Figure 5.22: A three-post turner's chair, mid 17th century. The crest rail once had a row of turned buttons, and the two outer spindles between the front stretcher and the seat have been removed to make room for the sitter's heels. This appears to have been done early in the life of the chair, and it is even possible that they were never fitted despite the holes having been drilled for them. The seat joints are ingenious and strong: one seat rail ends in a rectangular tenon that goes through the leg, the other in a round tenon that goes through it and the leg, thus locking the joint solid. This joint originated in Scandinavia. Courtesy Fiske & Freeman.

are generally made with three feete, but to distinguish them from the foure feete, you may terme them a three footed turned stoole or chaire." What Holme called "feete," we would call "legs." The words "turned" or "turneyed" and "thrown" or "throwen" were used interchangeably in the period to refer to work made on a lathe The word turner came from Latin and is southern in origin: throwen, from Old German *dhahan* and Old English *thrawan*, is Teutonic and northern, and therefore, as we shall see below, more appropriate for these chairs.

Thrown chairs are the earliest form of European chair. Some schol-

ars claim that they originated in Byzantium, and then spread via the Vikings to Scandinavia, from where they came to Normandy and England. Their presence in Byzantium is disputed, but their Scandinavian pedigree is not. The earliest surviving examples, dating from before 1300, are all in Scandinavian churches. A point of interest is that throwen chairs are one of the very few forms of English furniture to have originated in the north; most others came from Greece or Rome, or from the Far East, China in particular.

Turner's chairs may have been brought to England by the Normans, or more directly by the Vikings and

Figure 5.23: A four-post turner's chair, mid-seventeenth century. Every element except the seat has been produced on a lathe and many of the bobbins and rings spin freely. The arcaded decorations are halved rings whose outer edges are grooved to take the spindles on either side. The wings and back would have been draped with a cloth to keep the draughts at bay. Courtesy Fiske & Freeman.

other Scandinavian settlers. They came early. Illuminations in the Eadwine Psalter (1150) show arm chairs with knob turnings, and other records show that they were well established in the medieval and Tudor periods. As Randle Holme noted, they were of two forms: triangular or "three-post," and square or "four-post." The three-post form appears to be the earlier of the two.

During Queen Elizabeth's reign, joiners took over furniture making from turners and carpenters. The joined chair and stool replaced the turned chair and stool. "Turneyed" work was moved down the social scale. The combination of low status and rough use led to a low survival rate; not a single turned stool has survived from before the middle of the eighteenth century, and turned chairs, at least in comparison to wainscot chairs, are now few and far between. This was not always the case: in a widely quoted letter (August 1761), Horace Walpole, who wanted some to furnish his gothic mansion, Strawberry Hill, noted that, "Dicky Bateman has picked up a whole cloisterful of old chairs in Herefordshire — he bought them one by one, here and there, in farm-houses, for three-and-sixpence and a crown apiece. They are of wood, the Seats triangular, the backs loaded with turnery."

Today these massive, ornately turned chairs can seem striking unfamiliar, even a bit primitive. This is probably because, although most surviving examples were made in the seventeenth century, their form had remained largely unchanged since the Middle Ages. In the sixteenth

and seventeenth centuries the turned chair was to the yeoman farmer, the artisan, and the tradesman what the great, joined chair was to the landed gentry and nobility. It was the piece of furniture by which he could display his social status, and in which turners could show off their virtuosity: we might almost think that the turned chair enabled them to thumb their noses at the joiners: look what we can do that you can't!

Turner's chairs gave rise to forms that, on both sides of the Atlantic, became the common chairs of middling folk: windsors, ladder backs, or spindle backs, all of which were assembled from components turned on lathes without the benefit of mortise- and-tenon joints.

The American Connection

In England, joined chairs were more common and have survived in far larger numbers than turned chairs: in America, the reverse is the case. There are very few American wainscot chairs: most Pilgrim century chairs were turned. There are no American three-post chairs, although they were imported: the inventory of Richard Jacob of Ipswich, Massachusetts, (taken on Oct 4, 1672) includes "1 3 Square chair" valued at 4s. An elm example, with a history of ownership in Topsfield (near Ipswich), is now in the Smithsonian collection. But the best known is probably the Harvard's President's Chair, which was bought for the university by Edward Holyoke, who was president from 1737 to 1769.

Figure 5.24: Great chair, Suffield, Connecticut, or lower Hampshire County, Massachusetts, c.1700. Ash, modern rush seat. An old, possibly the original, woven ash splint seat is resting on a modern replacement. This chair well illustrates how a different society can erase the ostentation of figures 5.23 and 2.5 while retaining the basic form. Its new aesthetic, based upon simplicity, modesty, and functionality, is appropriate to a society founded in Puritanism and to a period that we now call the "pilgrim century." By permission of Historic Deerfield, Mr. and Mrs. Hugh B. Vanderbilt Fund for Curatorial Acquisitions. 2002.63. Photo by Penny Leveritt.

Four-post chairs were the norm in America. Two of the earliest and best known examples are the so-called Carver and Brewster chairs. Both were made in the mid-seventeenth century for the Pilgrim families after whom they are named, and are now in the Pilgrim Hall Museum in Plymouth. They are simpler and less massive than English turned chairs (whose posts were frequently of three inches diameter or more.) We might think that their simpler form was more appropriate to a society that had less need for clear signs of social status. The popular banister-back chair is their direct descendent.

The Chipstone collection contains the only known American three-post chair, but it is not a turner's chair. It is believed to have made in about 1640, by an immigrant millwright, John Eldekin who worked in Rhode Island and Connecticut. Only the front posts are turned: the construction of the rest of the chair derives from house-building techniques.

CHAPTER 6

Tables

Long Tables

As we noted in chapter 1, medieval tables were removable boards laid on trestles that were set up for each meal and taken down after it. *The Bokes of Keruynge and Curtasye* (c. 1485) instructed servants to "lay some of the tables on the floor and remove the trestles." The word "table" or sometimes "table board" referred to the top only, not to the combination of trestles and board. It also referred to anything rectangular and flat, such as picture and mirror frames and chessboards (chess pieces were sometimes called "table men"). Incidentally, this use of the word remains in, for instance, "timetable."

By 1550, one-piece tables were coming into general use. They were known as "dormant," or later as "joined." Their frames were joined and the tops permanently secured to them. They existed, however, much earlier: the hospitable Franklin in Chaucer's *Canterbury Tales* (1387-1400) possessed one:

> His table dormant in the halle always
> Stood ready covered at the longest day.

(The cloth covering it showed that it was always ready for use.)

It was some time before the whole piece of furniture became known as a "table." The Loseley Hall inventory in 1556, for example, lists "a table of Chestnut wt a frame joined to the same." Trestle tables continued in use alongside joined tables, probably for the lower-status diners in the main body of the hall. Certainly, the joined table from its introduction was a massive and impressive

Figure 6.1: A trestle table. The trestle table derives directly from the earliest form of demountable table. Now, however, the trestles are not free-standing but are joined by a stretcher that is mortised through them and held with oak wedge-pins. The plank top is cleated at the ends and is nailed to the trestles with large blacksmith nails. There are also blacksmith repairs to the feet. The table was probably made for a tavern in Oxfordshire in the first half of the seventeenth century. Courtesy John Andrews.

Figures 6.2a and 6.2b: A smaller trestle table. With well-shaped trestles and good wear on the central stretcher. The thick oak boards of its top are not cleated but are held by fillets glued into their long edges. Courtesy John Andrews.

piece of furniture, clearly designed to show the high status of those seated at it on the dais.

It was also designed to embody the family's longevity: like the house in which it was used, the joined table was made for future generations as well as the current one. One example makes this explicit: carved at the top of a leg is the legend "A Harelome to this Hous for Ever." The table is dated "163?"; the last figure has been lost (Edwards 1964:535-6). Some forty years later, John Evelyn made the point more generally: Tables, he noted, "were as fixed as the freehold." While the form of

Figure 6.3: A long table (9'6" long, 31" wide, and 31" high). From the first quarter of the seventeenth century with well-carved frieze and turned but uncarved legs that retain traces of the cup-and-cover form of the Elizabethan period. The wear on the stretchers shows that diners sat on both sides, and thus that it remained in use after dining in the hall went out of fashion. The wear also shows that six people sat on each side, allowing them only 19" of table each. Today diners are usually allocated 24" each (dining chairs from the eighteenth century onwards are 20" to 22" wide; joint stools were 16" to 18" wide). Courtesy Suffolk House Antiques.

long tables remained broadly the same, their symbolic function underwent an enormous change. From being movable, merely functional boards, they came to embody the permanence of the family's lineage.

FORM AND CONSTRUCTION

Long tables could be as long as twenty feet or even more, and were supported on four, six, or eight legs. The legs of the earliest examples were of a pronounced bulbous shape and were heavily carved. The friezes or aprons, too, were ornamented with gadroons and other motifs. On some tables the carving is on all four sides; on others it may be on three or even one. The tables did not stand in the center of the room and were not designed to

be seen from all directions equally. On the earliest tables, the floor-level stretchers were of T-section, but they were soon simplified to square or rectangular.

By the middle of the seventeenth century, the turnings had been simplified and the carving omitted. Long tables had become simpler and shorter; most were about seven feet long. By this period, single-board elm tops were often used instead of the two or three oak boards that were typical of earlier examples.

Some Elizabethan tables were fitted with draw leaves that pulled out from each end to almost double their length (see figure 1.2). Called "draw," "drawing," or "withdrawing" tables, they were the first examples of a form that was to become almost universal

Figure 6.4: A six-legged "table dormant" (12' 6" long and 3' wide). From the first quarter of the seventeenth century. It has a three-board top, and its legs retain the cup-and-cover form but are uncarved. Courtesy John Andrews.

— dining tables whose size could be reduced when not in use. They were, of course, derivations of the trestle tables that were dismantled after the meal. Indeed, the long table, or "table dormant," is the only form of dining table whose size is cannot be changed.

The beautiful expanse of patination on the tops of long tables is highly prized by today's owners, but in their period, tables were covered. Randle Holme talks of "... a Table, or square Table, covered with a Carpett. Some are covered with a carpet of Turky worke, or needle worke, and such like." For dining, expensive napery was used. Cardinal Wolsey's table was set with napkins of "Dyaper damaske worke with lozenges and birds-eyes" on a damask cloth "with flowers paned losingewise." It would seem probable that the "carpetts" would be replaced with linen for dining, but an incident in Pepys's diary suggests that this was not always the case. "So to Mr Crew's," he wrote, "where I blotted a new carpet that was hired, but

got it out again with fair water" (13 June, 1660).

Today, long tables are often called "refectory" tables, another Victorian misnomer that has stuck. Refectories were monastic dining halls, and the dissolution of the monasteries had been completed by Henry VIII by 1540, just before these tables appeared. In their day, they were called "joined," "dormant," "long," or "square" tables, or simply "tables,"

USE TODAY

The 28-30" width of the smaller long tables made it easier for servants to wait on the diners seated at one side, but they may appear uncomfortable for a modern dinner party when guests sit on both sides. Actually, there is plenty of room for place settings, but little for serving dishes or decorations in the center. In practice — and we have used one of these tables for thirty years — this has some advantages for guests do not have to converse with another through thick foliage or behind candle

Figure 6.5: A long table, c.1650 (84" long). A typical example of the smaller, simpler tables popular in the middle of the century. The base is oak, the top is a single board of elm. There is no carving, and the turnings are simple, as befits a piece made in the Cromwellian (Puritan) period. Courtesy Private Collection.

flames. A less conventional method of coping with the width is to use two tables side by side. It is easy to find two of closely similar length, particularly the 7' long tables of the mid-century, and their heights can easily be adjusted by invisible chocks under the feet. If the match is not precise, leave a 6" gap between the two. An arrangement like this may seem unconventional, but it seats ten diners in comfortable conversational range of one another and uses the tables almost in the manner for which they were designed, for the diners sit along one side only. We recommend it, and not just because we are dealers and would prefer to sell two tables instead of one!

People who have never eaten at a long table sometimes worry that the floor-level stretchers will be uncomfortable. This is not so. The stretchers' only disadvantage, if it is one, is that they can prevent chairs being tucked under the table when not in use. The backstools that many people like to use around a long table typically have low side-stretchers. Windsor chairs, which are also appropriate, have no such problem. But keeping the chairs around the table is a "modern" fashion dating from the reign of George III: it is better to arrange your backstools around the sides of the room (with perhaps one at each end of the table), as they would have been in the period. This allows the carving on

Figure 6.6: A six-seater gate-leg table, c.1680. The most frequently found larger size, with ends wide enough to sit at. Note the tongue-and-groove joint where the leaves join the table. The baluster-over-urn turning on the legs was also popular on gate-leg tables made in New York. Courtesy Fiske & Freeman.

their backs to be better appreciated and keeps their undecorated backsides properly out of sight.

COMMON FAULTS AND RESTORATIONS

By far the most common restoration is the replacement of the top. One clue to look for is the thickness of the boards: tops that were originally 1" to 2" thick have often been replaced with boards of an inch or less. Replaced tops often have a greater overhang at the ends. Otherwise, these sturdy tables have generally survived with only minor height loss and perhaps the replacement of one or two of their stretchers.

Gate-Leg Tables

The gate-leg table is the first intimate dining table. As we have noted, the Restoration brought many innovations in both lifestyle and forms of furniture: family dining, and the appropriate tables and chairs, was one

of the most significant. Everyday dining moved out of the great hall into a smaller chamber and became an occasion for family and guests, not for the whole household and retinue. Larger gatherings still dined in the great hall, but now they were seated in groups around a number of "oval" tables. Roger North, who visited the Duke of Beaufort at Badminton in 1680 noted that he had "nine original tables covered every day" and noted as peculiar that the Duke's own table was "an oblong not an oval." In their day, gate-leg tables were called "oval" or "round" to distinguish them from the long tables that they replaced. The oval shape of these new tables not only made conversation easier; it also did away with the rigid status distinctions that organized the seating at long tables.

FORM AND CONSTRUCTION

Most gate-leg tables are made of oak, though some are of walnut, and a few (the most expensive) of yew. Some-

Figure 6.7 A gate-leg table. A very attractive gate-leg table of about the same size and date as the one in figure 6.6. The spiral turnings, the fretted spandrels, and the great color make it worth at least twice as much as its plainer cousin. Courtesy William Smith Auctions.

times the frame is oak and the top elm or walnut.

Gate-leg tables have two drop leaves, usually D-shaped, that are supported, when raised, upon "gates." These gates are hinged or pivoted at both the apron and the stretcher (this, distinguishes them from the later "swing leg," which is hinged at the apron only.)

The raised leaf is supported on its outer edge by the outer stile of the gate, which extends above the rail. The leaf is thus supported only by the stile and the hinges. This structurally weak design often resulted in the hinges pulling out from the underside of the table. The problem was solved by giving the edge of the leaf a tongue that fitted into a groove running along the edge of the table top, thus taking the weight off the hinges. The rule joint, which served the same purpose and looked neater when the leaves were dropped, was introduced toward the end of the century. Tables with tongue-and-groove or rule joints are stronger, better looking, and thus more expensive than ones without.

All of the legs on gate-leg tables are block-and-turned. The blocks are at every join, enabling the joiner to use a strong mortise-and-tenon joint. Between the blocks are turnings of any combination of balls, rings, balusters, and spirals (a particularly desirable design.) The stretchers are usually of square section, often decorated with edge molding, though sometimes they are turned to match the legs (another desirable feature.) Some tables have a long, narrow drawer at one end. The design and extent of the turnings is an important value factor.

The fixed tops are usually of one or two boards, and the leaves of two or three: the widest board was at the hinge end, and a small, narrow one formed the curved tip of the D. These "tips" have often been replaced and even the originals can look like replacements because they were cut from different, narrower boards.

Gate-leg tables come in a wide range of sizes, seating any number between two and eight or even ten. The larger ones had two gates supporting each leaf and are known as "double gate-legs." They are hard to

SAMUEL PEPYS THROWS A DINNER PARTY

So my poor wife rose by five o'clock in the morning, before day, and went to market and bought fowls and many other things for dinner, with which I was highly pleased, and the chine of beef was down also before six o'clock, and my own jack, of which I was doubtfull, do carry it very well. Things being put in order, and the cook come, I went to the office, where we sat till noon and then broke up, and I home, whither by and by comes Dr. Clerke and his lady, his sister, and a she-cozen, and Mr. Pierce and his wife, which was all my guests. I had for them, after oysters, at first course, a hash of rabbits, a lamb, and a rare chine of beef. Next a great dish of roasted fowl, cost me about 30s., and a tart, and then fruit and cheese. My dinner was noble and enough. I had my house mighty clean and neat; my room below with a good fire in it; my dining-room above, and my chamber being made a withdrawing-chamber; and my wife's a good fire also. I find my new table very proper, and will hold nine or ten people well, but eight with great room. After dinner the women to cards in my wife's chamber, and the Dr. and Mr. Pierce in mine, because the dining-room smokes unless I keep a good charcoal fire, which I was not then provided with. At night to supper, had a good sack posset and cold meat, and sent my guests away about ten o'clock at night, both them and myself highly pleased with our management of this day; and indeed their company was very fine, and Mrs. Clerke a very witty, fine lady, though a little conceited and proud. So weary, so to bed. I believe this day's feast will cost me near £5.

- Diary, January 13th, 1663

find and expensive. The smallest are about 36" wide when open, and can be as narrow as 10" when closed, thus making them popular as side tables in smaller rooms or narrow hallways. The mid-sized tables that seat four or six are relatively common. A 36" or 40" gate-leg table serves well for cards or chess, or for an intimate supper for two. With only one leaf raised, the four- and six-seaters are also comfortable breakfast or supper tables for two. When placed in front of a window, with one leaf raised, a gate-leg table is ideal for a leisurely Sunday breakfast.

Gate-leg tables are comfortable for those seated at the leaves but less so for those at the ends. If you need to sit at the ends, make sure that the top is wide enough to allow your legs to fit comfortably between the legs of the table. This position is not recommended for the hostess, because getting in and out can be awkward: once in, however, the diner is more comfortable than might be expected.

COMMON FAULTS AND RESTORATIONS

Many gate-leg tables have had a variety of running repairs, restorations, and replacements. Replaced tops or leaves are particularly common. The hinge history is sometimes complicated, but it's the place to start. All marks and holes on the top, leaf, and apron should coincide: any that are not should raise red flags about the originality of the top or leaves.

Faults that devalue little: replaced or repositioned hinges, minor height loss, re-tipped feet, relined drawer.

Faults that devalue modestly: replaced tips on the leaves, repaired hinge breaks, re-cut rule or tongue-and-groove joints that shorten the leaf, replaced drawer.

Faults that devalue significantly: top and base associated (or "married"), replaced top or leaf (very common), a stripped and refinished top, rebuilt underframe.

Small Tables

Today's households have many more uses and places for small tables than did their Jacobethan counterparts: After the Restoration lifestyles gradually became more domestic, more human-scaled: in all except the wealthiest, most aristocratic, houses furniture became smaller and more intimate. Inventories tell us that a small table or two was customarily included in the furnishings of a bed chamber, where it may have been used for cosmetics and powders, or for the livery eaten at night or on awakening. Most of the small tables on the market today were made after Charles II had regained the throne.

Although Jacobethan furniture was highly decorated, it was never made for interior decoration alone. Today, on the other hand, we often use a piece of furniture to decorate a particular spot in our home. This practice began in the great houses of the Restoration period. Groupings of furniture composed of two torcheres, a pier table, and a mirror were made

Figure 6.8 A small gate-leg table, c. 1690. A common, versatile, and popular size. When closed it is only 12" wide, making it suitable for narrow hallways. With one leaf open it makes a fine end table, and with both leaves up, it is ideal for two people for supper or breakfast. Courtesy Fiske & Freeman.

for a specific position in the house. Most of this furniture is high baroque and made of walnut, often gilded or silvered; it is beyond the scope of this book. But it does indicate the start of the modern practice of considering furniture as part of the interior design of the home, and not just as functional pieces that were moved into position whenever they were needed.

Be that as it may, there is a greater demand for small tables now than there was then, and modern buyers have to compete for them. This may well explain the comparatively high price of joint stools: today they

Figure 6.9: A folding, or "credence" table, c.1630. The low points of the frieze have been restored: the originals had been cut off, not broken, presumably to increase knee-room. The drop finial is not original. Courtesy Fiske & Freeman.

are today versatile small tables, not seating furniture. Perhaps we should have included them in this chapter!

CREDENCE TABLES

So-called "credence" tables are one of the few forms of small table made in the first half of the seventeenth century. They have a folding top that is supported when open on a gate leg. When closed they are usually semi-circular or semi-octagonal. In the period they were known as "folding" tables; the name credence is, once again, Victorian. The more desirable examples have a low shelf at stretcher level, but on others the legs are joined by simple molded stretchers. Most have deep, ornately decorated aprons, a few of which contain a drawer. They are basically of the same structural form as the much lighter card or tea tables of the eighteenth century.

They would have been used for any activity that involved one person or a small group, and are more likely to have been found in the smaller parlors than in the main hall. They may have been used for intimate dining, for gaming (cards, chess, and dice games were very popular), for needlework, or for writing. For all their versatility, most are somewhat awkward to use: in the front their deep aprons and undershelves allow no room for people's knees. The early examples have a massive look, though they became lighter over time, and most owners today will use them simply as decorative side tables – a use that their design tells us was also important to their original owners.

Many have had considerable restoration, particularly to their undershelves and feet. Some have become pier tables due to the loss or removal of the folding leaf and the gate leg. But they are very beautiful, and they "look old"– their design is closer to the Elizabethan taste than to the modern, so any imperfections are readily and frequently forgiven.

SIDE TABLES

Side tables with a drawer, of a quite modern-looking form, became widely popular during the Restoration period. They usually have boarded tops with an ovolo molding around the

Figure 6.10: A folding table. With carved and applied decoration, mid-seventeenth century. An elegant example with the more sophisticated "card table" hinges that do not interrupt the surface when open. The hinges, the applied decoration, and the elegance all point to later date than the table in figure 6.9. Courtesy Suffolk House Antiques.

edge, though some have bread-boarded ends. Their most important features today are the turnings on the legs and the form of the stretchers. The most admired turnings are, in descending order, spiral, bobbin, and vase and ring. Bobbin and spiral turnings are likely to come from earlier in the period. The stretchers may be of box, H- or X-form. Box and H-form stretchers are most desirable when they are turned to match the legs. X-form stretchers are usually flat and shaped into simple Baroque scrolls: the best have a finial where they cross. An oak table with these stretchers is a vernacular inflection of the high-style tables made in walnut, often with marquetry tops. The more decorative the stretcher, the more desirable the table.

Side tables whose apron is finished on all four sides are called, for

Figure 6.11: A small, simple side-table c.1700. With a single drawer molded to imitate two, and with an unusually deep apron. Courtesy Fiske & Freeman.

Figure 6.13: A side table of high quality, c.1665. The top is an early example of veneering, the drawer and apron sides are inlaid, and the thumbnail molding of the top is repeated in the molding applied around the lower edge of the apron. The decorated ring turnings add life and interest to the bobbins. Courtesy Suffolk House Antiques.

Figure 6.12: Side Table c.1660. The bobbin turnings are lively, and the echo of their profile on the lower edge of the apron is a thoughtful touch. Courtesy Suffolk House Antiques.

Figure 6.14: A single drop-leaf writing table, c.1680. The double-gates allow plenty of knee-room. The turnings are as fine as are ever found in oak and have an elegance that is more typical of mahogany a century later. Courtesy Fiske & Freeman.

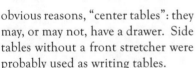

Figures 6.15: A coaching table, c.1700.
A fairly rare form whose comparatively small size (this one is 27" x 23" and is only 25" high) and its ability to fold flat support the idea that it was made to fit in a carriage. Today, their small size and the attractive form make these tables popular and pricey. Courtesy Fiske & Freeman.

obvious reasons, "center tables": they may, or may not, have a drawer. Side tables without a front stretcher were probably used as writing tables.

WRITING TABLES

Narrow tables with one drop-leaf and two gate legs were made to stand against the wall when at rest. In use, their double gate-leg action opened up a good space for the knees of their user: they were designed as one-person tables. They are now known as writing tables, and that was obviously one of their uses, probably their main one. In form these tables are often fine and light, as opposed to the more massive, masculine appearance of much early oak. Perhaps they were made for ladies, and may thus be seen as the beginning of a more "feminine" style of furniture. When folded, they are the narrowest form of side table and are therefore popular for use in small hallways or behind sofas.

COACHING TABLES

Coaching tables fold flat when not in use: they cannot stand on their own and must have been stored. They probably had many uses (the idea of a specific piece of furniture for each use was still alien, though it was taking root). Modern commentators explain their design by its ability to fit easily into a carriage for use in picnics or when traveling: hence the name "coaching table." It is one of the few small oval tables that you are likely to find, and you won't come across one often.

Figure 6.16: Walnut candlestand, c. 1675. An early candlestand that was made by a London cabinet-maker, as evidenced by the oyster veeners of exotic woods on the top and the dovetails by which the legs are joined to the platform base. Courtesy Fiske & Freeman.

Figure 6.17: Oak candlestand, c. 1680. With cruciform base, made by a rural joiner. Courtesy Victor Chinnery.

Figure 6.18: Candlestand, c. 1680. Ash with oak top, 24" high, made by a turner. The post could almost be a leg from a turner's chair. Courtesy Suffolk House Antiques.

Figure 6.19: A cricket table, c.1685. Of yew wood. The choice of timber, the crispness and fineness of the turnings, and the arched apron all identify this as a superior example of the form. Courtesy John Andrews.

CANDLESTANDS

Small, movable stands for candles or lamps are surprisingly late-comers. They existed before the Restoration, but were uncommon. Charles I's inventory (1649) records "two wooden painted frames to sett candlesticks upon." Randal Holme charmingly describes a candlestand as "a little round table, sett upon one pillar or post, which in the foote branches itselfe out into three or four feete or toes for its fast and steddy standing."

Candlestands became fashionable in the 1660s, and as with most

Figure 6.20: A cricket table. A more mundane but still attractive example of a cricket table from the turn of the eighteenth century. Tables of this form later became known as "drinking" or "alehouse" tables and were doubtless used in taverns. They were also found in dairies where they held the wooden cheese-molds. In fact, they were useful, general-purpose tables, as they are today. Courtesy John Andrews.

forms of furniture, they appeared first in the grandest houses. They were made of walnut, with spiral stems, and their tops were often veneered in exotic woods. It took a generation for the form to filter down through society and so the earliest examples made in country woods such as oak or elm date from around 1680. According to the inventories of the period, candlestands were quite common, but they are rare today.

Most of the early oak candlestands have a simple cruciform base made of two short crossed boards; others have three S-curved feet that are that are set into a small platform at the base of the stem, thus anticipating the familiar eighteenth-century form. The stems may be square-sectioned and crudely chamfered, or, more usually, turned with bobbin, vase-and-ring, or spiral turnings.

Their height may vary from 24" to almost 40". The lower ones rival joint stools in their suitability for a glass of wine beside your chair.

CRICKET TABLES

Cricket tables are three-legged tables with round or octagonal tops set on triangular joined frames. Three legs ensured a steady stance on uneven floors. Most were made for less wealthy households and have an appealing simplicity and sturdiness. Many have a shelf, either at stretcher level, or midway up the legs, and a few have a small cupboard or drawer. They were made throughout the eighteenth century and into the nineteenth, but the later forms do not have the floor-level stretchers of joiner-made furniture.

Their attractive name "cricket" probably does not derive from the three stumps used in the game but more likely comes from the cricket stool, a simple stool of wedged, not

Figure 6.21 Altar or center table, early seventeenth century. The reeded legs are "square-turned" (square, but profiled to imitate turnings) and retain the Elizabethan aesthetic. The rails and stretchers are attractively molded, and the top has "bread board" ends. Courtesy Suffolk House Antiques.

joined, construction that was widely used in cottages and farmhouses. Its low height made it well suited to sitting with the crickets in the hearth, where its user could bask in the heat of the fire while keeping below any smoke billowing out into the room.

ALTAR TABLES

Shorter long tables or larger center tables, about three or four feet long, are often called "altar" tables. This name may be correct and not a Victorian neologism. After the Reformation, the immovable stone altars of the Middle Ages were, by royal order, replaced with wooden tables. In her order of 1564, Elizabeth I required that the "... Parishe provide a decent table standing on a frame for the Communion ta-

ble..." and that it be brought from the chancel into the body of the church for communion (Chinnery 1979:224).

The local joiner would have made exactly the same sort of table for the local church as for the local houses, where one of their uses was for the first-stage of serving: they would have been placed at the opposite end of the hall from the dais for the kitchen servants to put the food that the retainers and henchmen in the hall would then distribute to the diners. Their greater than usual height of some does suggest that they were used for serving, whether the victuals were blessed or secular. Others, of more normal height, were general purpose small tables. Today, the larger, higher examples make good center tables in a library or large entrance hall.

CHAPTER 7

Serving and Display

Court Cupboards

In Elizabethan and Jacobean households, the court cupboard was one of the three most important pieces of furniture (the others were the tester bed and the great chair.) Court cupboards were fashionable between about 1550 and 1650.

In 1556, Sir William More of Loseley made a detailed inventory of his house and contents. On the dais in the hall stood his great chair, a lesser chair for Lady More, a long table and a "cup-board." Nearly a century later, in 1649, Randle Holme explains the use of such cupboards: "court cubberts, for cups and glasses to drink in, spoons, sugar box, viall and cruces for vinigar, oyle and mustard pot." The court cupboard was, in one of its uses at least, the sideboard of its period.

Its other important function was to display the master's "plate." The word plate referred to silver and gold vessels for drinking, eating, and serving. A display of it on the cupboard kept it handy for use on the high table, its beauty was an important part of the interior décor of the house, and it reflected and thus increased the low level of light in the room. But, as we noted in chapter 1, its main function was socioeconomic: plate was the accumulated savings of the master of the household; it was a public statement of his non-capital, liquid assets, and was thus a clear marker of his social standing. No wonder, then, that the court cupboards displaying it were such impressive and beautifully decorated pieces of furniture.

Open court cupboards (i.e., those designed primarily to display plate) were not made after about 1640. Cromwell's Commonwealth did not encourage the display of anything, not that there was much to display, for most of the plate had been melted down to finance the war against him.

Figure 7.1: A late Elizabethan court cupboard. With three shelves supported by carved cup-and-cover supports in the front and by plain supports in the rear. The top lifts to reveal a shallow storage compartment (see also figure 1.4). Courtesy Fiske & Freeman.

The open court cupboard was, literally, a cup board, i.e., two or three open shelves (boards) for the display of vessels for eating and drinking (cups). Some authorities spell "cup-board" with a hyphen to emphasize its original meaning over the modern one. The word "court" is the French or Norman word for short and has nothing to do with the royal household. The tops of court cupboards were display surfaces that were below eye level. They were usually covered with a cup-board cloth to enhance the display of plate.

Inventories also show that court cupboards were found in bed chambers, but what they were used for is never specified. Bed chambers were not as private as today's bedrooms, and guests were received in them, so perhaps they held any plate that over-flowed the cupboard in the hall along with, we might speculate, small boxes and cabinets for gloves, ruffles, lace, and cosmetics. They may also have been used for livery.

FORM AND CONSTRUCTION

The typical court cupboard of Elizabethan times consisted of three shelves (though two- or four-shelved examples were made) that were supported by elaborately carved pillars. Often there was a drawer in the middle shelf, and sometimes in the frieze at the top. More rarely still, the top lifted to reveal a shallow storage compartment.

The collector looks first at the shelf supports. The most desirable are figural — carved representations of men or women or of mythical beasts. The other desirable form is the "melon," a large carved bulb between finer ringed stems. This is often divided visually two-thirds of the way up so that it resembles a "cup-and-cover." The carving on these cup-and-cover supports, such as gadrooning or strapwork, often echoed the decoration of the silver cups that the cupboard displayed. The legs of the long table nearby would have been of a similar form and decoration, but table and cupboard would not have been made en suite — sets of dining furniture are a nineteenth-century innovation. Both the figural and the melon supports were typically surmounted by architectural capitols. The bulbous supports were not turned from solid wood but were built of four pieces of oak applied to the core piece. The rear supports were often of simple square section, some-times carved, but often left plain.

The decoration of the melon supports and of the fronts of the shelves or drawers encompasses the whole variety of Elizabethan and Jaco-bean motifs. On the supports we find strapwork, nulling, gadroons, tulips, and stylized foliage; on the drawers and shelves, nulling, guilloches, strap-work, and gadroons.

Standing Livery Cupboards

The basic form of the standing livery cupboard looks like a court cupboard with the upper shelf enclosed: we be-lieve that the enclosed portion was used to distribute livery. The absence of ventilation holes indicates that the cupboards were for distribution, not storage. The enclosed portion is usual-ly set back a few inches from the front and may be either straight-fronted or

Figure 7.2 A standing livery cupboard from the early seventeenth century. The upper tier is enclosed with a door flanked by canted panels, and the lower tier and the top are display surfaces. Courtesy Jud HartmannCollection.

canted. Collectors generally prefer the canted form (in which the central door is parallel to the front, and the two sides slant backwards). The earlier cupboards retain the carved supports in their front corners, later ones re-

Figure 7.3: A standing livery cupboard from the early seventeenth century. It is unusual in having the lower tier partially enclosed, though the bottom shelf and the top are still available for display. Courtesy Bob and Sara Hunt Collection.

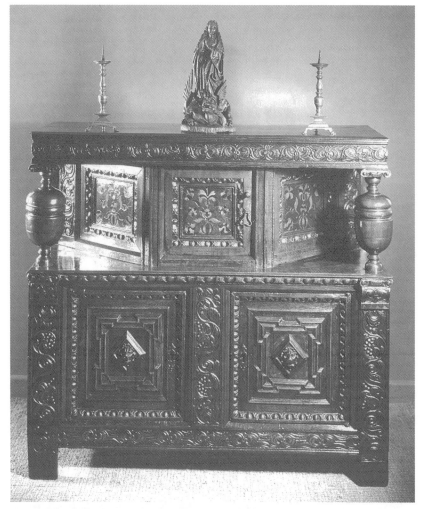

Figure 7.4: A fully enclosed court cupboard with a wide repertoire of decorative techniques and motifs. The upper tier, with its canted sides and central door, is typical of many standing livery cupboards, but the enclosed lower section is less common. Courtesy Suffolk House Antiques.

place them with a turned drop-finial hanging from the top corners (see p. 43). There is also a less common form in which both shelves are enclosed. All of these forms are often called "court cupboards," and we cannot be certain that all of them were always used for livery.

There is also a lighter form that looks more like an enclosed cupboard on legs than a court cupboard with one shelf enclosed (see "A National Style," p. 142 and figure 7.5). But both forms retain the lower shelf for display.

The cupboard front and door may be carved with any of the conventional motifs and figures, or may be inlaid with geometric, architectural or floral designs. The inlaid woods were light-colored holly or sycamore, dark bog oak, or green- or red-stained holly. The ground for the inlay was sometimes of lighter oak than the main piece and has now mellowed to a beautiful, honey color. Strings of geometric inlay, often of rope-twist or checkerboard design, were used in the frames around the panels, particularly in the north of England. Inlay increases the beauty and thus the value of the piece.

The cupboards in figures 7.1 through 7.7, in figure 1.4, and in the sidebar in this chapter are clearly related and show how widely the balance between display and storage can vary within a form. The categorical

Figure 7.5: A standing livery cupboard, c.1635. This form looks less like a court cupboard with an enclosed upper shelf, but it clearly serves the same purpose. Courtesy Private Collectiion.

break occurs with the press cupboard in figure 7.7. The press cupboard is not "court": its top is above eye-level and is usually made of rough, uneven boards; it was not designed as a display space. While it is convenient to call the par-

Figure 7.6: A court cupboard initialed "WS" and dated "1654." The lower tier is enclosed. Decorative carving is confined to the upper portion of the stiles, the shelf supports are turned, but not carved, and the rails and stiles are molded with a plane. The most decorative element is a long inscription extending over the top rails of the case and the door: "EXCEPT A MAN BE BORNE AGAINE HE CANNOT SE THE KINGDOM OF GOD." This cupboard exudes the Puritan spirit of the Commonwealth. Courtesy Suffolk House Antiques.

Figure 7.7: A press cupboard whose upper section resembles a standing livery cupboard. The not uncommon practice of calling this a "court cupboard" is confusing, for it is intended for storage only, not display. The less decorated press cupboards were probably used in the service rooms, but the more ornate ones were clearly placed in more public areas. Courtesy Fiske & Freeman.

tially enclosed forms "standing livery cupboards" to distinguish them from the open-shelved court cupboards, we should not assume that all of them were always and only used for livery. Many may have held the condiments and sauces, and many were in bedchambers. Though there is a general chronological change of priority from display to storage, there is no straight evolutionary line of development. Cupboards with more or less enclosed storage were contemporary with each other and would not have been viewed as more or less modern. The needs of the household explain the variations of the form better than a notion of evolution.

Court cupboards display treasured collections as spectacularly today as they did when they were new: today, however, their displays are more likely to be of delft or earthenware, or of pewter, brass or copper, than of silver or gold. Although they are often placed in dining rooms, using them for the condiments seems out of proportion to today's taste!

COMMON FAULTS AND RESTORATIONS

Many court cupboards have been restored or modified. Though they were solidly built and moved rarely, they were utterly out of tune with the eighteenth-century aesthetic, and as always, the unfashionable was little cared for and liable to modification. One common modification was the addition of a cornice to make the top look properly "finished" to a critical Georgian eye. The rough top boards were often replaced with smooth ones at the same time that the cornice was added. The Victorians also rebuilt and recarved court cupboards to their own tastes, often making smaller cupboards from original parts (see figure 10.5).

Faults that devalue little: pieced rear feet, reinforcements to interior and underneath, replaced interior shelves, rehung doors, minor repairs to carvings or inlay.

Faults that devalue modestly: replacement of some external shelf boards.

Faults that devalue significantly: later carving, rebuilding, replaced shelf supports.

Low Dressers

Low dressers, like gate-leg tables and backstools, became popular in the Restoration period as a result of the preference for more intimate dining. They rapidly replaced court cupboards, their predecessors. The court cupboard's ability to display plate was less relevant in a domestic-scale setting, and the new, more modest, low dresser was a more practical serving piece.

Before this period there was no dedicated piece of furniture for serving food from: any table may have served the purpose. David Knell (1988:150) quotes a wry account of a display on a "dresser." In 1628 John Earle, a future Bishop of Salisbury, wrote that the cook's

> best faculty is at the dresser, where he seems to have great skill in the tactics, ranging his dishes in order military, and placing with great discretion in the forefront meats more strong and hardy and the more cold and cowardly in the rear, as quaking tarts, and quivering custards, and such milk-sop dishes.

We should note that the word "dresser," as was usual in the seventeenth century, describes a function, not a form: the specialized form of a dresser came half a century later.

A NATIONAL STYLE

Standing livery cupboard, c.1640 (lower shelf lost).
Courtesy Jan and John Maggs Antiques.

The thistles sprouting from and surrounding the tree of life on this standing livery cupboard are Scottish: its form and carving, however, place it squarely within the English tradition. Why a Scots piece looks so English is an interesting question. Politically, the two countries had had the same monarch since the beginning of the century, but there were still deep divisions at the popular level, and a far longer history of mutual warfare than of alliance. We might reasonably have expected greater differences of taste and style than are actually apparent.

As this cupboard demonstrates, a distinctive British style emerged during the Jacobethan period. Within it, there were regional differences, but they were confined to details, generally the preference for certain motifs.

The similarity of furniture forms and decoration across the nation grew from a number of roots. Domestic life was broadly similar. Both Scots and English households needed a piece of furniture from which to distribute livery and on which to display plate.

Another unifying factor was the use of joinery as the method of construction. In English mannerism, the imagination of the carver was always constrained and inspired by the rectangular shapes of framing and paneling. The declining status of turnery (a result of the interaction of guild politics with cultural taste) is apparent in the quiet design of the legs, which, in contrast to their Elizabethan forebears, do not attract as much attention as the plate displayed behind them or the carving above them.

A NATIONAL STYLE CONTINUED

Less visible, but more influential, was the wide reach of the guild system, particularly its training of apprentices. As many as 60% of the London-trained apprentices went to the provinces to work, and we may assume that when they became masters, the prestige of their London training ensured that they attracted the best of the local apprentices. The combination of the 1563 Statute of Artificers (see p. 25) and the prestige of the London guilds was another factor in the dissemination of a national style.

So was the monarchy. Henry VIII and Elizabeth I both used the royal court to unify a previously fractious nation. And the Stuarts continued the process. The London court bound regional aristocrats to a single center from which they took its tastes and behaviors back to their local communities. The constant movement of lords and their retinues between the court and their estates disseminated London taste across the country and established the city as the center of all that was fashionable.

The national style that grew out of the unifying forces of a common lifestyle, the monarchy, the guild system, and the dominance of London was itself, as we saw in chapter 3, the result of a particular selection and interpretation of international motifs. From a European mother tongue, a British style emerged as a distinct language, and within it regional differences were "spoken" as local dialects.

America had no monarchy and no court; it had no guild system; and it had no single city as dominant as London. Pilgrim-century America lacked three of the unifying forces of England. As a consequence, regional differences are more strongly marked in American furniture, and more important to the American collector.

CONSTRUCTION AND FORM

Low dressers come in two forms: open and enclosed. Open low dressers are long and narrow, typically between five and seven feet in length, and rarely more than twenty inches deep. They generally have three drawers (sometimes four) that, in the earliest versions, are decorated with applied geometric moldings. A few have a row of small spice drawers along the back. They may have two, three, or four legs in the front, but only two in the back. The front legs of the early examples are turned with the vase-and-ring turnings typical of the period, although some legs were flat boards silhouetted to resemble turnings. After the turn of the century, pad-footed cabriole legs became the fashionable supports. The curves of these new "Queen Anne" legs were often carried over into the scalloping of the apron below the drawers. The William and Mary versions were usually finished with a straight molding beneath the drawers. The two rear legs are straight and rectangular in section.

The depth of the drawer section allowed the legs to be strongly constructed, so stretchers were not a structural necessity, but they were sometimes fitted. Side stretchers are

Figure 7.8: Open low dresser from the last quarter of the seventeenth century. This narrow depth of this form limits its use to dressing and serving the food. It could not have held the sort of display that Earle describes. A wider table must have been used, possibly a larger version of the one shown in figure 7.9 or an altar table like the one in figure 6.21, or even, we might speculate (without much evidence), a long table that was no longer used for dining. Courtesy Fiske & Freeman.

Figure 7.9: Enclosed low dresser. Of about the same date as the one shown in figure 7.8. Enclosed low dressers are usually 2-3" deeper than the open form and may well have been used to display the food before serving. Courtesy Suffolk House Antiques.

common, front stretchers less so.

In enclosed low dressers the space under the top row of drawers was enclosed with three cupboards or an arrangement of drawers and cupboards. The enclosed form was not as common in the seventeenth century, but it gained popularity in the eighteenth and lasted into the nineteenth, whereas the open form is not often found after about 1750.

Low dressers are popular today. In a less formal dining room both the enclosed and open forms still serve their original purpose. The narrowness and visual lightness of the open form makes it more versatile, and it is often used in the entrance hall or behind a sofa in the living room.

NAMING

The term "low dresser" is a modern one that distinguishes the form from the high dresser that has a rack above it for storage and display. The high dresser was particularly popular in Wales, so it is often, in fact usually, called a "Welsh dresser," although the form was also made in England. Sometimes a low dresser is called a "dresser base": this is confusing, for the term dresser base ought to be confined to a high dresser that has lost its rack, as many have. The word "dresser" refers to its use for dressing the food with its final garnishes just before serving. The low dresser evolved into the sideboard. In the period, as is often the case, the word "dresser," or its French form *dressoir*, referred to function rather than form: any side table could serve as a dresser. Our current practice of categorizing a piece by what it looks like was not followed by our forebears: for them a piece was defined by its use.

Figure 7.10: A side table with cupboard that had many possible uses. One may well have been as a "staging post" between the kitchen and the table where the kitchen servants placed the dishes that the henchmen would serve to the diners. It may also have been used as a dresser, and, in practice, the two uses may have been combined. Courtesy Suffolk House Antiques.

Figure 7.11: A high dresser. Dating from c.1690, this is one of the earliest examples of a high dresser, or dresser with rack. The flat legs that copy the profile of William and Mary baluster turnings are interestingly echoed in the blind-fret carvings between the drawers. Courtesy Suffolk House Antiques.

Figure 7.12: A "hooded" dresser made in Denbighshire early in the eighteenth century. The projecting hood on the rack is a sign of its early date. Courtesy Suffolk House Antiques.

The high dresser, incidentally, did not derive from the low dresser. Both derived from the rough kitchen "dressing board." The high dresser remained in the kitchen, where its rack and often potboard, provided functional storage. The low dresser moved into the dining room, where, today, it has been joined by its higher, if younger, cousin. In Welsh farmhouses, the cooking and eating areas were in the same room, so the true Welsh dresser was multi-functional: it was used for kitchen storage, displaying china, and serving food.

COMMON FAULTS AND RESTORATIONS

Many a low dresser is actually the base of a high dresser that has lost its rack. Check for any plugged holes or shadowing at each end where the feet of the rack will have rested. But remember that racks were often secured to the wall and merely rested on the base, the absence of screw holes does not necessarily mean that the base never had a rack. Check also to see if the backboards extend behind the top, allowing the backboards of the rack to fit neatly above them, but remember that many racks, particularly in the earlier dressers, did not have backboards, in which case the backboards of the base will be flush with its top. Dressers with potboards almost always had racks. The base of a high dresser can be a useful and quite attractive piece of furniture, but it should be less than half the price of a low dresser.

Faults that devalue little: Rear legs ended out (common), minor replacements to drawer moldings or lips. Many with only two front legs have developed a sag over the years: whether this is a fault or an attraction is a matter of taste. A shrinkage gap between two boards has often been closed by moving the rear board forward and adding a narrow strip to the back — this has no effect upon value, and, for some, will make the piece more attractive.

Faults that devalue modestly: relined drawer(s), replaced rear legs, one top board (usually the rear one, for some reason) replaced, missing side stretchers, later backboards added to rack.

Faults that devalue significantly: replaced front leg(s), replaced top, reduced length to two drawers (on low dressers in particular).

CHAPTER 8
Beds

Privacy and Prestige

Tudor and Elizabethan beds were big. Paul Hentzner visited Windsor castle in 1578 where he saw "a chamber in which are the royal beds of Henry VII. and his queene, of Edward VI., and of Anne Bullen (Boleyn), all of them eleven feete square, and covered with quilts shining with gold and silver." Even these royal beds were dwarfed by the bed made for the Duke of Burgundy for his marriage to Princess Isabella of Portugal in 1430: it was a magnificent 19' long and 12' 6" wide.

The Great Bed of Ware, at 10' 8" square, was also huge, though made in about 1595 when the size of beds was decreasing. Its overlarge size gave it instant fame. Shakespeare wrote *Twelfth Night* in 1601, only half a dozen years after the bed was made, yet he could rely on the audience getting the point when he made Sir Toby Belch refer to "as many lies as will lie in thy sheet of paper, although the sheet were big enough for the bed of Ware."

The maker of the Astley Hall bed (figure 8.1) was like many of his colleagues in recognizing that furniture of this scale needed to be treated as architecture: what he was really making was a private chamber within a public space. The scale of the bed had two effects: its exterior displayed the wealth of the owner. amd its interior provided him and his wife with privacy.

In the Elizabethan period, as today, privacy was one of the most important purchases the wealthy could make. Throughout the sixteenth century, both bed and dining chambers became increasingly common in the great houses. The bed chamber afforded a welcome personal space that was used for more than sleeping and dressing: inventories show that it was often equipped with furniture designed for writing, needlework, or chess-playing. The bed chamber was also used to receive high status guests and, particularly in the later seven-

Figure 8.1: A magnificent Elizabethan bed. It is full of architectural features that literally made it a room within a room. With curtains closed, it provided luxurious privacy, when open it was an object of magnificent display. On a bed such as this, the woodwork would have equaled the hangings in importance. The plain panels indicate the depth of the bedding. Courtesy Astley Hall Museum and Art Gallery.

teenth and early eighteenth centuries, as a place where the lady of the house could entertain and gossip with personal friends. Whether the Jacobethan bed was located in a private chamber or was still in the great hall, its drawn curtains gave the master and his wife more than draft-free warmth: they provided a personal space that nobody else in the household enjoyed. The interior was a place of privacy and privilege.

The exterior of the bed made a comparable statement of power and prestige. It symbolized social power both by the wooden structure of the bed itself and by the textiles it supported. Today, the wood has survived while the fabric has not, so we tend to think that the magnificence of the bed was the product of the joiner and

carver. In the period, however, textiles were more significant than wood.

Hangings and Bedstuff

Many of the silks and damasks that surrounded the bed were imported and thus more notable by far than the woodwork, which was made locally. The inventories of the period invariably emphasized the hangings. Chinnery quotes a typical one:

> A bedsteade of cutwirke, A teaster and vallans of black and cremysine velvet and frindged with cremysine silke and golde, Curtains of red and yallowe changeable taffetie, One downe

BEDS ROYAL AND HUMBLE

"A bed Royall, the vallance, curtaines (turned about the posts) and counter pane laced and fringed about: with a foote cloth of Turky worke about it: the Tester adorned with plumbes, according to the colours of the bed."

"...a Bed with blanket of Cadow or Rugg: or covering: the sheets turned down, and boulster...this is a bed prepared for to lodge in, but having no Tester. Such are termed Truckle beds, because they trundle under other beds: or being made higher with ahead, so they may be set in a chamber corner, or under a cant roofe, they are called a field Bed or cant Bed. If it be soe, that it may have a canapy over it (that is a half tester) then it is termed a Canapy bed: to which belongeth curtaines and Vellance.

In the base of this square ly's a bed staffe, of some termed a Burthen staffe."

From Randle Holme: *An Academie or Store House of Armory & Blazon* (1649).

---

bed, a bowlster, ij pillows, and ij wollen blancketts, One red rugge, one quilte of cremysine sarcenet... (1624)

The Victoria and Albert Museum has refurnished the Great Bed of Ware (figure 1.6) with hangings in a very similar color scheme: bright reds and yellows were the height of fashion. Randle Holme's list of "Things usefull about a Bed and Bed-chamber"

and the inventory of Paget Place are both typical in paying closer attention to the hangings, carpets and needlework than the furniture (see "Bedding and Bed Chambers" and "Bedding the Great Bed").

The bedstuffs, or as we would call them today, the bedding, were as excessive as the hangings. Ralph Edwards (1964:30) tells us that the most luxurious medieval beds consisted of "a straw or wool pallet, two featherbeds, sheets (sometimes of silk), blan-

BEDDING AND BED CHAMBERS I

From Randle Holme: *An Academie or Store House of Armory & Blazon* (1649):

Things usefull about a Bed, and bed-chamber.

Bed stocks, as bed posts, sides, ends, Head and Tester.
Mat, or sack-cloth Bottom.
Cord, Bed staves, and stay for the feet.
Curtain Rods and hookes, and rings, either Brass or Horn.
Beds, of chaffe, Wool or flocks, Feathers, and down in Ticks or Bed Tick.
Bolsters, pillows.
Blanketts, Ruggs, Quilts, Counterpan, caddows.
Curtaines, Valens, Tester head cloth; all either fringed, Laced or plaine alike.
Inner curtaines and Valens, which are generally White silk or Linen.
Tester Bobbs of Wood gilt, or covered suteable to the curtaines.
Tester top either flat, or Raised, or canopy like, or half Testered.
Basis, or the lower Valens at the seat of the Bed, which reacheth to the
ground, and fringed for state as the upper Valens, either with Inch fring, caul
fring, Tufted fring, snailing fring, Gimpe fring with Tufts and Buttons, Velum
fring, &c.

The Chamber

Hangings about the Rome, of all sorts, as Arras, Tapestry, damask, silk,
cloth or stuffe: in paines or with Rods, or gilt leather, or plaine, else Pictures of
Friends and Relations to Adorne the Rome.
Table, stands, dressing Box with drawers, a large Myrour, or Looking glass.
Couch, chair, stooles, and chaires, a closs-stool.
Window curtaines, Flower potts.
Fire grate, and a good Fire in the winter, Fire shovel, Tongs, Fork and
Bellows.

kets, another feather-bed, and overall, an embroidered quilt, often trimmed with fur." This huge pile was kept in place by bedstaves that slotted into holes in the top of the frame. Generally, these holes are found only on the most impressive beds, indicating that the depth of the bedstuff signaled the height of the sleeper's rank. Bedstaves were also pushed betwen the bedding and the bed frame. People slept in a semi-sitting position, propped on bolsters leaning against the headboard.

William Harrison tells us with his customary pride that during Elizabeth's reign comfortable bedding, which he calls "lodging," spread to the farmers and artisans:

The second is the great amendment of lodging, for (said they) our fathers (yea) and we ourselves (also) have lien full oft upon straw pallets, covered onlie with a sheet, under coverlets made of dagswain or hopharlots (I use

---

BEDDING AND BED CHAMBERS II

From An Inventory of all maner of stuff remaining in Paget Place, St Clement Danes at London 15th February 1552:

In My Lord's bed Chamber

a joined bedsted of walnuttree
a testor of gold sarsenet imbroded and double valanced
5 curtaines of blew and orange sarsenet
a bed of downe wt. a bolster
a chaire of black velvet – a chayre of needle worke
a square table wt. a grene carpet
a cupbourde wt. a grene carpet
a red mantle ij paires of tables
a chesse bourd, a deske of ivory
a little square stole, a fote stole
th' angings of arras of the story of David 4 pair

---

their owne termes), and a good round logge under their heads in steed of a bolster, or pillow. If it were so that our fathers, or the good man of the house, had within seven years after his marriage purchased a matteres or flockebed, and thereto a sacke of chaffe to rest his head upon, he thought himself to be as well lodged as the lord of the towne, that peradventure laye seldom in a bed of downe or whole fethers; so well were they contented, and with such base kind of furniture: ...Pillowes (said they) were thought meete onlie for women in childbed. As for servants, if they had any sheet above them, it was well, for seldome had they anie under their bodies, to keepe them from the pricking straws that ran oft through the canvas of the pallet, and rased their hardened hides.

The passage echoes his account of the social diffusion of plate on court cupboards (pp.11-13), and we should note that he makes no mention of the furniture, if any, upon which this bedding was laid.

Tester Beds

While Jacobethan home owners took great pride in colorful, expensive bed hangings and in deep piles of bedding, they were far from neglectful of the bed itself. They loved carved and inlaid oak so much that the opportunity of a large bedhead was just too good for the carver and his patron to pass up. The Great Bed of Ware, for instance, has magnificent hangings, but its carving and inlay is by no means overshadowed.

After the Restoration, the beds of the court and the nobility became notable only for their textiles, the wood was nothing but a supporting

Figure 8.2: A tester bed, northern English, dated 1663. The form and decoration have been much simplified from the bed pictured in figure in 8.1, but its structure is basically the same. The upper panels are carved with arabesques, strapwork, and an arcade and the date; the stiles are carved with running guilloches, and the other rails and muntins with scrolls and lozenges. The lower panels are plain because they would have been covered by the pillows. The tester is fully paneled and has running guilloches on the stiles and a molded cornice. The headboard, footboard, and tester clearly show their close relationship with the fronts of joined coffers. Courtesy Camcote House Collection.

BEDDING THE GREAT BED

Kate Hay, a curator at the Victoria and Albert Museum, describes how late sixteenth-century bedding has been recreated in authentic detail for the Great Bed of Ware (see figure 1.6):

> The first layer of the bed would have been hemp rope, strung between the holes in the bedstock. To prevent the mattress sinking through the stringing, a bedmat made of plaited rushes was laid over the top. Three mattresses would probably have been used, the lowest filled with woollen flock, the second with feathers, and the top with down, making a very soft sleeping surface. One mattress is covered in striped ticking, with a period pattern, and two with plain canvas. Bedstaves, long wooden poles, were pushed down the sides of the bedstock to keep all the matttresses in place.
>
> Two plain linen sheets have been specially woven. These were authentically made in narrow strips of just under two feet wide which were then sewn together. The bed has been provided with a bolster, and eight pillows. Four of the pillows have linen pillow cases, and four have blackwork embroidery. On two of the pillowcases the design of the embroidery copies a pillowcase in the Museum's collection and on the other two the design has been taken from contemporary design drawings in the way embroiderers would have worked in the 16th century.
>
> Two woollen blankets were made using traditional methods, with a twill weave and woven blue stripes at the end. Over these was laid a quilt. The quilt is in 'shot sarcenet', a silk with the warp and weft in different colours so that it shows different colours as the light falls from different directions. The pattern for the embroidery on the quilt is taken from a 16th century quilt in the Museum's collection, and the two colours are 'carnation', (pink), and green, one of the most popular colour combinations recorded in inventories. The counterpane was often used to display luxurious fabrics, such as the one used for the bed, a fabric woven in wool with linen and gold thread. This also follows the pattern of a 16th century textile in the V&A's collection.
>
> The curtains and valances are in bold stripes of red and yellow say, a twill-woven wool. This was chosen because it is very frequently mentioned in inventories of the period, and was the most popular colour combination in inventories from the south of England. The curtains also have a woollen fringe trim.
>
> The final result shows the bed as closely as possible to its probable appearance when it was first used in the 1590s.

Figure 8.3 A half-headed bed. This is a younger cousin of the tester bed. The headboard has similar plain panels surmounted by carved ones, and the foot posts echo faintly the form of those that support a full tester. The rope-stringing for the mattress is clearly visible. These ropes needed to be tightened frequently to ensure a comfortable night's sleep: our good-night wish "sleep tight" derives directly from this necessity. Courtesy Suffolk House Antiques.

Figure 8.4 A half-headed bed . This is of simpler form than the bed shown in figure 8.3, though it still bears clear traces of the full tester bed. This example has a paneled footboard. Low half-headers like this were often made to fit under the eaves in an attic bed chamber, in which case they were called "cant beds." Courtesy Suffolk House Antiques.

frame completely covered by the hangings. These beds of state grew to fifteen, or even seventeen, feet high, with hangings that might have cost as much as £7,000. Below this exalted social level, however, traditional joined beds remained popular, and their testers, headboards, and posts were often masterworks of carving. It is these beds, usually called "tester beds," that interest today's collector.

Tester beds consisted of three parts — the tester, the headboard and the bedstock. Testers were paneled and carved ceilings over the beds. In medieval beds, the tester consisted of curtains hung from the ceiling of the room: it was not structurally part of the bed at all. By the Elizabethan period testers were wooden, and were integrated into the bed: they were supported by the headboard at one end and, at the foot, by freestanding posts. Curtains hung from rods around their three sides to make the room within a room.

The paneled headboard was divided visually into two. The upper part was ornately carved and inlaid in the height of fashion, but the lower part was of undecorated paneling because the pile of bedstuff was deep enough to cover it. The division between the two sections was often marked by a ledge that could hold a rushlight or candle.

The bedstock, or, as we would call it, the bed frame, was of sturdy oak, pierced horizontally with holes for the ropes that held the mattresses, and, in some cases, vertically with holes for the bedstaves. At one end it was attached to the headboard, and at the other was supported on low posts that stood inside the large posts supporting the tester. During the seventeenth century, these four posts became integrated into two that supported both the frame and the tester.

Tester beds became less fashionable as the seventeenth century progressed. They also became smaller, sized for one couple only, less elaborate, and more appropriate for private life. By the second half of the century they had shrunk to the extent that many have had to be enlarged for modern use. But even in their modest, simpler forms, tester beds remain magnificent pieces of furniture.

Half-Headed Beds

As beds became simpler, they increased in numbers, so that more people in the household could sleep in one. Beds without testers appeared in the seventeenth century, either in more modest households or for those of modest status within larger ones. These "half-headed" bedsteads looked much like our modern beds — a carved headboard that rose two or three feet above the frame, and simple posts at the foot. An inventory of 1635 lists "one halfeheaded bedsteddle with one small featherbed and feather boulster, one blanket, one ould coverlid." The more modest bedstead had more modest bedstuff.

Truckle or Trundle Beds

Truckle beds were low frames on wheels that rolled under the great bed in the day time. A 1611 inventory lists

Figure 8.5: Joined truckle bedstead, Welsh, seventeenth century. Courtesy Victor Chinnery.

Figure 8.6: A seventeenth-century oak cradle. We must imagine a typical bedchamber containing a tester bed for the master and his wife, a truckle bed under it for a servant and possibly an older child, and a cradle for the baby. There is little wonder that the master and mistress liked to draw the curtains around them and enjoy their own little room within a room. Courtesy Jan and John Maggs Antiques.

"a greate posted bedsteadle, a trundle-bedsteadle to it;" and an inventory of 1660 explains further: "little trundle beds under the greate beds, which were for the gentlemen's men." In 1668 (June 11), Pepys recorded in his diary, "[We] came about ten at night to a little inn, where we were fain to go into a room where a pedlar was in bed, and made him rise, and there wife and I lay, and in a truckle-bed, Betty Turner and Willett." The absence of privacy is underscored when we remember that Pepys and Deb Willett, his wife's maid, had a long affair that caused many marital arguments. Few truckle beds have survived: they were of no use in later households. We must surely, however, regret the passing of the word "trundlebedsteadle"!

Restorations

We have yet to see a seventeenth-century bed on the market that has not been modified or restored. Resizing to fit a modern mattress is more than acceptable, other restorations should be judged on their quality. Look particularly at the molding around the tester — this has often been added, embellished, or restored, and the height of the bed has often been reduced.

Looking-glass with walnut veneered frame and fretted crest, English, c.1690.
Courtesy George Subkoff Antiques.

REFLECTION

This looking-glass concludes the century and the historical sections of this book. The man or woman looking into it was Jacobethan, but the face reflected back was the new face of modern England.

Before the Restoration, mirrors were small and rare: After it both their size and their popularity increased dramatically. Mirrors began to be used to reflect light as well as people: they were used publicly to enlarge rooms as well as privately to enhance self-image.

The English glass industry began during the reign of Elizabeth, but it was not until 1621 that it began to make looking glasses. Until 1660 it struggled weakly. In that year, the monarchy was restored, and the Vauxhall glass works was established. In 1664 the Worshipful Company of Glass Sellers and Looking-glass Makers was formed, and by 1675 it had as many as 85 members. The industry was booming.

In Tudor England, "glasses to look in" were known, but rare. A few glass mirrors were imported at great expense from Venice. English-made mirrors were of polished steel and were covered by shutters when not in use to prevent oxidization. Mirrors are seldom mentioned even in Elizabethan inventories. In this period a "glass" could be made of either glass or steel. In 1588, for instance, the furnishings of Leicester House included "three great glasses, one standing in a verie faire frame, with beares and ragged staves on the top, with a steele glasse in it, the other II of cristall."

Living as we do in a society of the self and of self-image, it is hard for us to imagine a life in which almost nobody could see what they looked like. In the Tudor period, only the wealthiest could see their own reflections, and then of their faces only. Very few people can ever have seen a full-length reflection of themselves. The wealthy were dressed by servants, and their clothes were determined more by their social position than by their personal taste: appearance was a matter of status, not of personality. The communal society of the Middle Ages had little sense of the individual self and thus little need of looking glasses. Checking one's appearance before going out in public was unnecessary. It is impossible to have a sense of self, if one can never see oneself: self-reflection has dual and inter-related meanings.

Technology and social desire run hand in hand. Medieval society lacked mirrors not because it was unable to produce reflective surfaces, but because it did not need to: technological incompetence is not an adequate explanation. The looking-glass industry and the sense of the individual grew in parallel. It is no coincidence, therefore, that the late seventeenth-century boom in looking-glasses came at the same time as the boom in personal portraiture. Nor is it surprising that the fashion for mirrors and portraits flourished when people chose to dine with individual place settings around an oval table that was "convenient for seeing and conversing."

Looking-glasses, portraits, and individual table-settings were typical of the culture that concluded the century-long transformation of English society that we have traced in this book. They were the material objects that enabled people to live comfortably with their new, individualized identities. They are the antiques that form the threshold of modernity.

PART III

An Owner's Guide

CHAPTER 9

Restorations and Repairs

It is hardly surprising that furniture that has been in daily use for four hundred years has needed some repairs along the way. Oak is a very hard wood that actually gets harder as it ages, so some pieces, a remarkable number of them in fact, have survived in close to their original condition. But many have needed one, at least, of the three Rs of the antiques business – restoration, repair, or replacement. Antique dealers are not always noted for the precision of their language, and you may find these terms used interchangeably, or with fuzzy areas of overlap. But they do refer to different ways of keeping antique furniture alive and useful. As an antique buyer, you will often be faced with deciding how much restoration you are willing to accept and at what price you are willing to accept it. Knowing what the terms mean will help make that decision.

Restoration refers to the attempt to return a damaged antique to its original condition so skillfully that on the surface the restoration is undetectable. The restorer uses either new wood that he makes look old, or old wood salvaged from another antique. The line between restoration and faking is a fine one: good repairs are open and honest. Restoration can, however, be both invisible and honest: in what is sometimes called "museum restoration" the restoration to the visible surface is invisible, but inside or underneath the restorer leaves clear signs of his work. The owner and the furniture historian will always know what has been done: the guest will see only a piece in perfect condition.

A *repair* enables a damaged object to continue to serve its original function. Often a repairer uses no new material but glues or mends breaks in the original. On oak furniture, you will sometimes find wrought iron reinforcements or "blacksmith" repairs. Most are out of sight, but if they are visible, you may well consider them not blemishes, but charming signs of the history of the piece. A good repair is unobtrusive, but not invisible.

There is also a category of repairs that we should consider maintenance. Maintenance is the equivalent taking your car in for its regular service; it corrects the wear of normal usage and keeps it in good working order. The rails that side-hung drawers slide on have often been replaced, and the grooves in the drawer sides may have had fillets inserted to keep the drawers sliding smoothly. These are acceptable maintenance: reaching for your socks in the morning should not involve a struggle with a recalcitrant drawer. *Relining* refers to the rebuilding of the interior of a drawer, which some may consider maintenance, and others restoration.

Replacement usually refers to the replacement of working parts, such as handles, hinges, and latches, that have worn or broken with use, but it can also refer to the replacement of a complete component, such as a door, a lid, or feet. In these cases it may be called restoration. Not much seventeenth-century hardware has survived, and old replacements are not considered too major a fault: only a serious collector, for instance, would decide not to buy a bible box because its hinges had been hand-wrought in the mid-eighteenth century.

These terms are not always used consistently or clearly. There is a gray area, for instance, where replacement overlaps with restoration: a strip of geometric molding on a drawer front may be legitimately labeled "replaced" or "restored." A new lid on a coffer may also be labeled "replaced" or "restored," as may the bun feet on a chest of drawers. In these cases, we strongly prefer the word "replaced." It indicates that the whole element has been replaced and that there is no evidence in the piece itself to tell us if the replacement is restoring the piece to its original form, or if it is "enhancing it." New bun feet, for instance, may have replaced stile feet, in which case they are not restorations, but enhancements. The replacement is an attempt to increase the financial value or visual appeal of the chest. Enhancement is fakery.

How Much Is Too Much?

Of course, a piece in original condition is always preferable to one that has been restored. Restoration is always a negative, but not all restorations are equally detrimental. There is no one-size-fits-all formula to distinguish between acceptable and unacceptable restoration, but there are a few guidelines to help you decide.

Rule of thumb #1: Rarity outweighs restoration. One helpful criterion is what we might call the "time-till-the-better" principal: How long will it take you to find an equivalent in better condition? There is no point in buying a coffer with a replaced lid because you'll only have to walk down the street to the next dealer to find two or three whose lids are original. No point, that is, except the price — which should be low, very low. On the other hand, you may find a wainscot chair with rare and distinctive carving and a replaced front stretcher. If you have been looking for five years to find carving that catches your eye in the way that this does, don't let another five go by with a void in your house, your heart, and your collection. Buy the chair, enjoy the wonderful carving, and rest your feet on the stretcher.

Rule of thumb #2: Frequency is a good excuse. You should also consider how common the restoration is. If the normal history of a piece frequently produces the need for restoration, the restoration becomes almost maintenance and is not too serious a drawback. For instance, the rear feet of case pieces have often been "tipped," "ended out," or "pieced" (you will come across all these terms). This is because the back feet stood against the wall on the dampest part of the stone floor where they rotted: their normal history frequently produces the need for ending out. The rear feet of backstools, too, have often been tipped because they have taken most of the weight. Restoration to the rear feet of these pieces is not significant and may almost be considered maintenance. On the front feet, however, the increase in visibility and the decrease in frequency makes the equivalent restoration considerably more significant.

Rule of thumb #3: Significance increases with the distinctiveness of the restored part. The components of a piece of furniture are not equally important to its identity. The most distinctive feature of a court cupboard may be its gadrooned cup-and-cover supports: restoring or replacing them is far more significant than replacing the top boards — nobody buys a court cupboard because they love its top boards. The element that first attracts your eye is the one that, above all others, should be original. Elements that make one piece stand out from others should always be original. If a distinctive feature has come from the hand of the restorer, it may be an enhancement, not a restoration. Beware.

Rule of thumb #4: Quality counts. The skill of the restorer should approximate as far as possible that of the original maker. If the carving on a restored part is stiff and mechanical, it will offend you more and more as time goes by (a possible exception to this rule is a farmhouse repair whose crudity may have a charm of its own). Good restoration is not only technically skillful; it is sympathetic with the original. Assessing the quality of the restoration is similar to, and as important as, assessing the quality of the original.

Rule of thumb #5: Aim high (most of the time). Always buy the best you can afford and occasionally the best that you can't! The anxiety of writing a check that is larger than you had planned will fade quickly: the pleasure of a great antique will last forever. We've lost count of the number of times that a customer has told us, "I paid more than I'd planned to for it, but I'm so glad that I did!" Or, more sadly, "I had the chance to buy one a few years ago, but it was more than I could afford at the time." Equally common is the lament on the other side of the coin: "I bought it because it was cheap, and I've regretted it ever since." As dealers, we, too, have to remind ourselves to buy the best that we can afford, and sometimes need to screw up our courage with the old adage: "Good stuff ain't cheap, and cheap stuff ain't good."

If you think that you may turn into a serious collector, set your stan-

TO BUY OR NOT TO BUY, THAT IS THE QUESTION

Restorations always complicate matters for the prospective buyer. The seat on this backstool has been replaced. Ordinarily, this might put you off the purchase because backstools with their original seats are not too hard to find. But this is no ordinary backstool; it is dated.

Applying the time-till-the-better principle will lead you to conclude that you will probably never see a dated backstool with no restoration in your lifetime. Dated backstools really are as rare as that. Possibly this is because backstools were often made in sets, unlike wainscot chairs, boxes, and press cupboards, which were all quite frequently dated. A date seems to require a unique object.

Another reason to overlook the replacement is that the seat of a backstool is not one of its distinctive features: nobody buys a backstool because they love its seat. The seat is made of old wood and resembles the original fairly closely: the replacement is not jarring.

TO BUY OR NOT TO BUY CONTINUED

The little form pictured above poses different problems. It has good carving on the apron, legs, and stretchers. It is early, dating between 1590 and 1610. It is unusually small — able to seat two children, or, at most, a mother and child. It is rare, attractive, useful, and many years will pass before you find another like it.

But it has lost one stretcher, and its seat was originally the lid of a small coffer: it is a marriage. The seat has been attached with pegs and rosehead nails, the iron of the nails has oxidized into the wood, staining it black, and the color match on top and underneath is excellent: the new seat has probably been in place for two hundred years. But it has notched ends like a lid instead of a molded edge like a seat. The notches will remind you every time you see them that it is a lid, not a seat. It also has the scar left by the hasp. But still, the distinction of the piece lies in its small size and its carving, not in its top. The lost stretcher poses another dilemma — whether to restore it or live with the loss. In its present condition, both the loss and the lid are visually apparent in the way that the restored seat on the backstool is not.

Buy the backstool without hesitation. Think carefully about the form. If you are furnishing your home with oak, leave it, unless it happens to fit your space exactly: in which case, buy it and restore the stretcher. If you are a collector with a gaping hole in your collection that only a small, late Elizabethan form can fill, then you won't need us to advise you to buy it, live with its faults and enjoy its good bits while you hunt for the perfect example.

The replaced seat on the backstool has devalued it by 25% or less; the problems with the form have devalued it by 50% or more.

Figure 9.1: A wainscot chair. This wainscot chair has obviously lost its stretchers. The front legs have been tipped with small blocks to level the chair so that it can be used. The blocks are unobtrusive, but make no effort to approximate what was there originally. An earlier generation of collectors would probably have restored the feet and stretchers to their original appearance. Most collectors today, however, prefer losses to restoration, provided that the losses do not make the piece unusable (compare the replaced seat on the backstool in the sidebar). Courtesy Private Collection.

dards high and buy only pieces with minimal or no restoration. Put your limited funds into one great piece in preference to three lesser ones.

But buying the best is not the strategy for all people at all times. If you are furnishing a room or a house on a limited budget and don't want to sit on packing crates for too long, you will be far better off buying a number of well-restored "furnishing grade" antiques instead of new furniture or reproductions. If you want "the look" at an affordable price, then buy a piece that has been restored to its original appearance. Do not, however, buy one that has been adapted or modified: as your eye improves, its wrongness will grate on you. It will also, if you care about such things,

signal your ignorance to a knowledgeable guest!

Properly restored antiques are valid and legitimate. A restored antique does not lose half its value as you carry it out of the shop. A restored antique will never become merely second-hand or old fashioned. When you want to upgrade, as sooner or later you will, a restored antique will help you afford the piece you really want. Your dealer may take it in part exchange or he may offer to sell it for you. If you send it to auction, you will probably get your money back, and may even make a small profit. You will be so pleased that you spent your limited money on less expensive antiques instead of on reproductions at comparable, or even higher, prices.

Figure 9.2: The back of a coffer. Dry seventeenth-century oak can sometimes look almost new, as with the back of this coffer. Courtesy Fiske & Freeman.

Rule of thumb #6: There are no rules. When buying early oak, you will have to make your own decisions about the extent of restoration you find acceptable. This will be your decision, and yours alone. A home furnished with antiques expresses the character of its owners in a way that one furnished with mass-produced furniture cannot. The choice of antiques is individual, and so is each home that they furnish. To buy early oak furniture you have to think for yourself — there are no trendy magazines to tell you what is in this month and will be out next. Different people buy early oak for different purposes and with different priorities. Just be clear of your own, and don't apologize for them. The only inviolable rule is: make sure that you know what you're buying. Always ask the dealer to go over a piece in detail with you, showing you what has been done to it to keep in good working or-

der. You should not be afraid of restorations, but you should know about them.

You will also meet the thorny question of losses. Some collectors prefer loss to restoration. They prefer not to have the lost ear of a wainscot chair restored. They prefer their linenfold coffer to tilt backward on the rotted-out ends of its rear feet. For them, a loss is an authentic effect of history, and restoring a lost component compromises the integrity of the piece. This is a purist attitude and contrasts directly with the belief that an antique should look to its current owners as closely as possible to what it did to its original ones. Neither is correct, neither is better. One may suit you, the other may not. The decision is yours. The only hint we can give is that the more specialized the piece, the more likely that a collector will prefer loss to restoration. And, of course, vice versa.

Problems that Might Not Be

Let us end this section on a more positive note. Sometimes things can look wrong that are not. When you turn a piece around or upside down, you may think that the boards or panels look too new to be true. Oak that has never been finished, waxed, or oiled can be light grey color whose clean, dry surface may mislead you into thinking that it must be less than three hundred years old. The secondary woods of eighteenth-century furniture, primarily deal, darken with age, and if they have spent most of their lives in rooms heated with coal fires can become almost black. Oak that has aged in a dry, smoke-free atmosphere goes silvery grey. It can, however, darken: all wood ages differently according to the conditions through which it has lived.

The second problem that might not be is a piece of wood that shows evidence of previous use. Seasoned oak was never wasted: it got harder and harder to find as the seventeenth century progressed. Pieces from older furniture and joiners' mistakes were never discarded but were reused unobtrusively. If everything else is right except some inappropriate peg holes or carving, do not necessarily assume the worst. The joiner never expected you to inspect the inside and underneath of his work as carefully as you are now doing!

CHAPTER 10

The Victorian Goths

English Gothic

The Gothic Revival that flourished for most of the nineteenth century and well into the twentieth was responsible for a lot of new, remade and recarved Jacobethan furniture. Some of it is nearly two hundred years old, and some of it was quite well made. All of it can be a trap for the unwary lover of early oak.

"Gothic" was the most generic term, but the style was also called medieval, Tudor, Elizabethan, or Jacobean. The linguistic imprecision indicates clearly that any historical differences between the early medieval and the William and Mary periods counted for little. The gothic revival was the result of nostalgia, not history.

The English taste for the gothic has waxed and waned but has never died. In the early eighteenth century, just after early oak went out of fashion, it was in deep hibernation. By the middle of the century, however, it had revived, and Chippendale, for instance, designed many Georgian pieces of furniture in the gothic taste. At about the same time that Chippendale's *Director* was at its most influential, Horace Walpole was enlarging, transforming, and furnishing Strawberry Hill, his small 1698 house in Twickenham, until it became "the most celebrated Gothic house in England." In 1764 he wrote *The Castle of Otranto*, the first gothic novel in English. While the gothic may not have been the dominant taste of Georgian England, it was by no means an unusual or eccentric one.

There was an important stylistic difference between Chippendale gothic and Walpole gothic. Chippendale was a Georgian: his gothic is confidently eighteenth-century contemporary. It drew from the past but made no attempt to reproduce it. Chippendale's gothic motifs were incorporated into eighteenth-century forms, just as his Chinese motifs were thoroughly anglicized. Walpole, on the other hand, was more like the Victorians: his gothic was an attempt to

FASHIONABLE GOTHIC

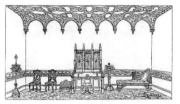

A general view of the interior of a drawingroom fitted up and furnished in the gothic style.

"The tracery of the ceiling should be of oak, or of stucco painted in imitation of that wood. The fillets and flowers should be gilt; the panels painted blue, and the ornaments of the cornice also gilt. The dado should be of oak, painted and gilt. In this Design are shown two different varieties of chairs, a piano-forte, a music-stool, a music-desk, a Canterbury, a sofa, a fire-screen, and a footstool. We need not express an opinion of this interior; for every reader, we think, must be pleased with it. Even the studies of furniture which it affords are interesting; the Gothic piano-forte and music-stool, with the Canterbury on the left hand, and the music stand on the right; the Gothic couch, with its footstool; the two beautiful chairs; and, finally, the firescreen, all claim attention, and are each separately worthy of study." – From J. C. Loudon, *An Encyclopedia of Cottage, Farm, and Villa Architecture and Furniture*, London, 1833.

The pride in Loudon's account of his designs is as typically Victorian as the inaccuracy of his "gothic."

revive the look and feel of the past as a counterpart to the present.

It was Walpole's gothic that swam into the Victorian mainstream. While Chippendale's gothic appealed to a few members of the upper classes, Victorian gothic was popular throughout the middle-classes. Henry Shaw's book, *Specimens of Ancient Furniture*, published in 1836, was one sign of this mainstream gothic; the huge popularity of Sir Walter Scott's romanticized medieval novels was another. Architects were at least as influential as writers: Pugin re-designed the Houses of Parliament in the early 1840s into the apogee of Victorian gothic. Similarly Walter Scott had his baronial home, Abbotsford, transformed into an Elizabethan mansion. All over Eng-

land, churches, schools, railway stations, town halls, suburban villas, and country cottages were decorated with pointed arches, knobbly spires, and tall, narrow windows. Ironically, genuine medieval churches had their interiors remodeled to fit the Victorian idea of the gothic: medieval gothic was too sparse and austere.

This historically eclectic, inaccurate, and over-enthusiastic gothicism may be seen as symptomatic of a country that had become artistically disoriented by the rapidity of its rise to an imperial power, and whose cultural center of gravity lay in the middle-class, and not, as previously, in the court and nobility. A stylistic link between the two great queens of England, Elizabeth I and Victoria, must

Figure 10.1: A recarved coffer. A good example of Victorian scratch carving, done with a V-shaped chisel. Two immediate giveaways are the lunettes on the lid (no coffer of this form had its lid carved) and the doubly ludicrous date. The coffer was made one hundred or more years after the inscribed date, and no date in the period was identified as AD, because there was never any need to distinguish it from BC. The wobbly form of the figures is an arrogantly childish idea of the "primitive." On first glance, the lozenge may appear more authentic, but the longer we look at it, the less authentic it appears. The lines are uneven and uncertain, there is an aesthetic mismatch between the lozenge and the roundel inside it. The channel molding around the lid, and along the upper and lower edges of the front is authentic: its edges and texture show how much older it is than the harshly scratched lines of the Victorian "improvement."

have seemed reassuring to its citizens. While classical Greece, Rome, and Egypt had lent the prestige of their antiquity to the styles of late-Georgian England, the Victorians turned to the gothic. Unlike the classical, the gothic was appropriately English, reassuringly Christian, self-confidently magnificent, and not too intellectually demanding.

Carve-Ups and Make-Ups

The Victorians believed that the age they had brought into being was the most advanced, and therefore the best, that human history had yet produced. While this self-confidence, dare we say arrogance at times, may have had some basis in reality, it certainly did not apply across the board. One instance

Figure 10.2: A recarved coffer. Another example of Victorian enhancement, showing a high degree of dexterity coupled with an absence of taste and an ignorance of the period. The comedy of errors includes: The designs overrun the edges of the panels: the panels were removed for carving, and the carver forgot that they rested in grooves in the inside of the frame. The surface and not the sunk ground is matted. The background is not taken out or sunk. The outlines of the designs are too fussy, with too many different curves. The leaves are not stylized enough. The "palmette" has two different types of leaf and a peculiar branched root. None of the surface of the design, except for the scrolls, is left flat. The carving on the top and bottom rails is authentic, and so is the channel-and-groove molding on the stile and the central muntin: the foliate carving, however, is not. Courtesy Fiske & Freeman.

where it had no justification was their belief that their "Jacobethan" taste was better than the Jacobethans'. This led them to "improve" seventeenth-century furniture whenever they felt so inclined. And when faced with an undecorated surface, the inclination was strong. Many a panel or board that the seventeenth-century joiner had left plain was "improved" by a Victorian carver. We might say that Victorian taste suffered even more acutely

than the Jacobethans themselves from aesthetic agoraphobia, the fear of an open space and a plain surface.

Fortunately, such carving is fairly easy to identify. The Victorians did not try to reproduce seventeenth-century decoration exactly — they were decorators, not historians — so they freely translated it into a Victorian aesthetic. Their carving was guided by their own sense of the gothic, which had far more to do with the nineteenth century than the seventeenth. To our eyes, the Victorian chiselers simply got it wrong, but in their terms, they were improving upon the original, not slavishly copying it. Carving was a popular pastime for both men and women. There were evening classes and magazines devoted to the skill, and many plain oak pieces, both of the period and later, were re-gothicized.

But the Victorians did not stop at carving. Genuine Jacobean furniture had to be scaled down to fit the smaller and much more crowded rooms of the Victorian middle classes. So it was remade without compunction. This remaking often involved combining genuine seventeenth-century parts with new ones, or applying period decorations onto newly constructed pieces.

In his *Encyclopedia of Cottage, Farm and Villa Architecture and Furniture* (1833), J.C. Loudon recommended that

> the exterior of chests or wardrobes might be rendered curious, and highly interesting... by covering them with them with Elizabethan, Dutch, Louis XIV or Francis I ornaments, which are now to be purchased in abundance...Wilkinson of Oxford Street, and Hanson of John Street, have extensive collections of Elizabethan and Dutch furniture and carvings, from which a judicious compiler of exteriors might clothe skeleton frames, so as to produce objects of curiosity and interest, at a very trifling expense.

Figure 10.3: A Victorian carve-up. A good eighteenth-century oak bow-front corner cupboard has been carved with Victorian Jacobethan motifs. It is now neither seventeenth nor eighteenth century, but uniquely nineteenth. The running guilloches and their floral interiors bear little resemblance to their seventeenth-century equivalents (cf. figure 3.6h).

John Andrews (1989:374) tells us of Victorian hobby magazines advising, "Take an old chest, knock out the carved panels and put to one side, cut off the legs..."

One of the most obvious "make-ups" that you will come across frequently will be that of the hall bench or settle. Many of these were made up using a mixture of new and recycled parts: the front of a coffer and the stiles from a backstool could be com-

Figure 10.4: A Gothic make-up. A make-up whose reconstruction is impossible to date. The linenfold panels are from the mid-sixteenth century, the hinges from the seventeenth, and the four corner stiles are of old wood that is probably from the period. Raised or fielded panels, however, are not found until late in the seventeenth century and can never be contiguous to linenfold. In the period, narrow shelves were only found in enclosed cupboards: open shelves were for display, and this is far too narrow for that. This piece is trying to be a dressoir from about 1525, but in a dressoir the cupboard is two-thirds of the way up, and its display top usually has a back and sides. This make-up is a catalog of errors, but it can still be, as here, a useful and decorative piece in the kitchen, better looking by far than any modern equivalent.

bined to make the back, and if more height was needed, another coffer could be plundered, or new rails and panels made, and, of course, carved, to fit. Another common make-up was a hat and coat rack: the front of a coffer, or sometimes just the top rail of one, was fitted with wooden pegs and hung in many a Victorian entrance hall (coffers, it seems, were particularly rich resource-banks of re-usable parts).

Made-up wainscot chairs were also popular. Wainscot chairs epitomized Elizabethan England and were widely reproduced. Some were made up by combining parts from different dilapidated chairs, others ranged more widely for their component parts. One we saw recently was typical: its seat rails and front legs were once the top rail of a coffer, its back panel was probably from a bedhead, the stiles looked like the rails of another coffer that had been topped with bizarre finials, and so on. The Victorians lacked neither imagination nor skill.

When completed, their new antiques were stained black and var-

Figure 10.5: A Victorian make-up. A Victorian reconstruction of about seven-eighths the size of a seventeenth-century cupboard. The doors and central panel of the upper tier are period but they have been set in a case that has been scaled down to fit a crowded Victorian room. The disproportion becomes obvious when we look for it. The gadrooning on the central drawer is good, the other decorative details are less convincing. The horizontal applied split spindles are inauthentic and of a different period than the gadrooning.

nished. The black, shiny finish is easily recognizable today and was obviously exactly what the Victorians thought Jacobethan furniture should look like, for they applied it to genuine pieces as enthusiastically as to their own. From the genuine pieces it should be removed: under it there is often a good old surface that patient waxing can restore to its true beauty.

Reproducing and Renaming

The rapid growth of mass production enabled the Victorians and the generation that followed to make revival pieces in large quantities and at low cost; the style was fashionable well into the 1920s. Dining suites were especially popular, but large cupboards, bookcases, and coffers were also made. Fortunately, any resemblance of these factory-made reproductions to seventeenth-century furniture is remote, and even in the dark from fifty paces they are unlikely to be mistaken for the real thing. The one exception is the gate-leg table: Victorian copies can resemble originals quite closely and often require careful inspection.

The Victorians not only made up pieces of gothic furniture, they also made up gothic names. Medieval churches were found in many English villages and towns, so the ecclesiastical and the gothic became almost synonymous in the Victorian mind. Consequently they freely stuck ecclesiastical names onto domestic furniture in order to make it adequately gothic. To long tables they gave the name "refectory," even though the tables were made after the monasteries and their refectories had been dissolved. They called a table box a "bible" box, and a joint stool a "coffin" stool. The folding table they not only called a "credence" table, they used it as one: according to Chinnery (1979:223) they took these household tables into churches to hold the bread and wine for communion and then renamed them to imply that their Victorian use was, in fact, the original.

You may be able to accept a piece that a Victorian carver has enhanced, provided that the proportion of enhanced to original carving remains low. Make-ups or revival pieces, however, are so "wrong" as to be difficult for an educated eye to live with in a home furnished with early oak (although, if you have a wry sense of humor, you may find a coffer-front coat rack useful in your hall). A collector may include any or all of them in a chamber of horrors warning him of the worst, and a furniture historian may find them interesting as specific forms of the gothic in the history of English taste. But the home furnisher will simply find them ugly.

Gothic, after all, was originally a term of abuse. It was coined in the Renaissance to describe the barbaric and uncivilized times that are still sometimes called "the dark ages." The Goths, along with the Vandals, sacked Rome and destroyed Roman culture: their name was therefore appropriately used to describe cultural vandalism. For most people, the term "Victorian Gothic" refers to a stylistic revival: for the lover of seventeenth-century furniture, however, what it revives are the echoes of what "gothic" meant to those who first coined the word.

CHAPTER 11

Provenance and Patina

Provenance

A provenance is the documented history of a piece. With early oak, this is rarely complete: in the seventeenth century, furniture was far more common than documents. Some pieces have stayed in one house for their whole life and can be matched with a listing in an early inventory or even a bill of sale, but these are few and far between. A good provenance enriches the historical value of a piece, particularly if it includes an association with a historical figure or event. It also underscores the authenticity of a piece by ensuring that it is not a fake, though it does not guarantee the absence of restoration. It also sets the piece apart from other, similar ones and thus creates its uniqueness. All these effects increase the value of an antique. A good provenance puts the price up.

But what makes a provenance good? The main factors are:

Time: The further back the provenance stretches, the better.

Status and celebrity of previous owners: The more famous the family through which the piece has descended, the better. In the case of an individual owner, again, the more famous the better. But do question the source of a person's fame: an owner whose fame rests on achievements of historical importance will add more value than one whose fame rests on his or her ability to charm the masses. The former is, in general, a more durable fame; it will be as important when you come to sell the piece as when you bought it.

Collection and exhibition history: The value of a piece is enhanced if has been in a major collection or has been exhibited in public or is illustrated in a reference book. But beware here: some early collections were put together according to criteria that differ from today's. In particular, some early collections allowed condition to weigh less against form and historical significance: items from them sometimes have more restoration than today's collector would find acceptable. Personally, we think that our contemporary emphasis on originality of condition has gone a bit too far — we have had customers reject pieces because of restorations that were, in our opinion, of far less significance than the importance of the form. But we live in today's conditions, we don't create them, and we can't do much to change them. Museums, too, deaccession many items that they would never buy today: An accession number from a prestigious museum does not tell us if the piece deservedly spent its whole time in the back of the basement.

Commercial history: Old sales documents from a long-established and respected dealer or auction house add a little, but not too much, to the sense of authenticity, and therefore the value.

Patina

Patina is the mellow look of an old surface that has been exposed to light, air, and dust for three hundred years or so, and that has been untouched except for the cleaning, polishing, and handling that are part of everyday life. Collectors rightly value it highly, because it is the best single guarantee of authenticity — no refinish or restaining can reproduce it exactly. Like a good reputation, patina once lost can never be regained.

Patina is the best provenance, and it has been valued as such for a long time. In his book *Culture and Consumption*, Grant McCracken tells us that patina was highly valued in Tudor England. The Tudor period saw the fixed society of medieval Europe loosening up under the influence of the Renaissance. Upward social mobility became possible for the first time. Possible, but not easy. The manners books of Elizabethan England, explained that it took five generations to make a gentleman. As Lord Burghley, Queen Elizabeth's private secretary, put it: "Gentility is nothing else but ancient riches." Furniture that had been in the house for generations showed, through its patina, that the family was properly "gentle."

The new money of the emerging mercantile class enabled its members to furnish their homes with new furniture and silver, but it was new: It lacked patina. To speed up their five-generation wait, these upwardly mobile Elizabethans would, whenever possible, buy old furniture and silver, that is antiques with patina, from the established gentry. And thus, we may surmise, the antiques business was born, and then, as now, patina was at the heart of it.

Similar factors may well underlie the importance that today's collectors place on "original finish." Today, however, their concern is less to establish their social status than to preserve, and participate in, a sense of heritage. Heritage is the history that is not written in books, but is carried by artifacts.

PATINA AND PREFERENCE

This American joint stool, as we might expect, closely resembles the English examples shown in chapter 5, though the seat overhangs further. But its dried, old surface reminds us that there is no single definition of a "good patina" or even of "original surface." Indeed, the terms refer to different surfaces on each side of the Atlantic. To put it simply: the English like their furniture polished and the Americans don't. To the English eye this stool might look neglected and sorry for itself. To the American, however, it has that desirable surface that is the product of the passage of time alone, with no help, or interference, from the human hand.

Joint stool, New England, 1660-1710. Oak, pine. This stool was found in Chiltonville, at the southern end of Plymouth County, Massachusetts. By permission of Historic Deerfield.

American patina is the effect of hundreds of years of air and light and dust, and nothing else, upon the surface of furniture. English patina, on the other hand, is a surface that has been waxed once a year for three or four hundred years. One produces a grungy, open-grained patina that varies depending on the original treatment of the surface: the other results in a smooth, deep luster. The differences, of course, lie on the visible surface: underneath and inside, both the English and the Americans look for the same oxydization. Whichever form it takes, patina is an effect that only time can produce. Both forms signal authenticity, but their signals are different.

Today's transatlantic differences of taste must have historical roots. It may be that in England servants were more numerous, and they had time to perform less necessary work, such as polishing furniture: they produced what we now call "country house condition." Some colonial Americans had servants, too, but fewer, and they worked at the more essential housekeeping tasks. One was a leisured, settled society, the other a working, developing one. Well-polished furniture in England was a sign of social position: it fitted right in to the highly developed class system. In America, where the class system was denied (though far from absent), the "neglected" surface might have signaled a more Puritan, Yankee ethic — a dislike and distrust of embellishment.

Climate may have had something to do with it as well. England's damper climate is not good for wood, and wax is a good damp-proofer.

Incidentally, and contradictorily, the preferred patina on pewter is exactly the opposite: Americans like theirs cleaned and shiny, whereas dull and grimy is the English taste.

Figure 11.1: Joined armchair, Yorkshire, 1650-1700. This chair-back shows excellent patina, whose color ranges from a chocolate through a rich chestnut to a pale honey. The color and wear show exactly how the owner leaned against the back. The history of its use is written on the chair itself in a way that guarantees its authenticity. Courtesy Fiske & Freeman.

It is the history not of great men and historic events, but of ordinary folk and their everyday lives. Our heritage lies, to put it simply, in the things we keep.

The patina on the things we keep makes that heritage visible and tangible. Patina links the current owner of an antique with all its previous ones into an unbroken chain of heritage that stretches from the past, through the present, into the future. A refinish, or patina lost, reduces the symbolic, and thus monetary, value of an antique because it breaks this chain. A piece's provenance is its documented history that accompanies it: patina is the history that is written on the piece itself.

CHAPTER 12

Care, Maintenance, and Investment

It is clichéd, but true, to say that we never own our antiques outright, but hold them in trust for future generations. We have a responsibility to our antiques, to ourselves, and to the future to look after them well. Fortunately, this is neither difficult nor onerous, and it can be rewarding. Giving your early oak its annual waxing can be an important part of the pleasure in owning it. You get to know your antiques more closely when you're polishing them. In fact, the relationship can become quite intimate; and as with any intimate relationship, rushing spoils it, and good music improves it.

Originally, sixteenth- and seventeenth-century oak was finished with wax. A block of beeswax was rubbed over it, and then it was buffed. This method was improved when the wax was dissolved in warm turpentine to make a paste. Turpentine came from pine tree resin. Applying this repeatedly over time allowed the wax to penetrate the porous surface of the wood, and built up a lustrous sheen that was the basis of what now we call patina. Later in the seventeenth century, furniture was oiled rather than waxed: a mix of turpentine and linseed oil was applied very thinly and repeatedly over a period of months. Linseed oil dries very slowly, but it does provide a good waterproof finish for people with the patience to use it. It also darkens wood over time. What we need to note here is that the original finishes were all achieved with natural products and elbow grease. And we should never use anything different.

John Evelyn's book *Silva, a Discourse of Forest Trees*, published in 1662, shows the importance given to polish in the seventeenth century:

There is a way so to tinge oak after long burying and soaking in water which gives it a wonderful politure [polish] as that it has been frequently taken for a coarse ebony. The process of putting walnut into a hot oven so that the oils in the timber are heated and rise to the surface so that they can be used to polish the surface.... Ebony, Box, Larch, Lotus, Terebinth, Cornus, etc, which are best to receive politure, and for this linseed oil or the sweetest nut oil does the effect best." (Edwards, 2000:172)

Normal Care

Apart from obvious general advice, such as to shield furniture from direct sunlight and to avoid subjecting it to rapid changes in heat or humidity, there are routines of maintenance that will preserve early oak's aesthetic and investment value.

Polishing with wax is the only way to maintain the patina of early oak. Use nothing but wax and elbow grease. If your piece already has a good finish, it will need little maintenance: dusting weekly with a soft cotton cloth will be enough. Never use oils, silicones, or other synthetics: if you can spray it on, don't. You will need to wax only when the dusting fails to restore the shine, about once or twice a year at the most.

Always use a black or dark brown wax in preference to a clear one: it fills any grain that may have opened slightly, and any residue will not dry unattractively white. Wax provides the best look, but not the toughest surface. While it protects well against water and alcohol spills if they are wiped up fairly quickly, it is useless against heat, and it scratches easily. Treat your antiques with common sense and a little bit more care than furniture whose "finish" is a synthetic wood-grain veneer. Never put a hot dish on a wax surface. Use coasters under glasses, and mats under flower vases. Pad the rough bottoms of earthenware with little felt discs.

When you need to wax, wax thinly and wait. The two most common mistakes are using too much wax, and buffing too soon. With a soft cotton pad, apply a thin coat of wax — just enough to smear the surface. Many professionals prefer a pad of 0000 steel wool. Leave it for an hour or more, preferably more. Buff with a clean soft cotton cloth, or a lambswool bonnet on your electric drill (the softer the buffing material, the better the shine). Use the most comfortable motion — circular, along, or across the grain, it doesn't matter which, but always finish with long strokes along the grain.

If you have used too much wax and the surface remains blurry, put more on! This may seem to run against common sense, but a new light coat will soften the excess of the previous one and enable you to wipe it off with a cotton pad or paper towel. Remove the softened wax immediately, before it starts to harden again. Or you can use mineral spirits or turpentine as a stronger softening agent. But try wax first.

Polishing carving requires a bit more effort. The single most helpful tip is to use a brush instead of a pad, because bristles can get into crevices that a pad cannot. Always use natural bristle, never synthetic. Cut the bristles of a one-inch paint brush to a length of about an inch, and tape the metal ring of the brush to avoid any danger of scratching the wood. Or use a toothbrush. Use the brush to work a little wax into the carvings and crevices. Clean off any excess with a soft cloth, paper towel, or another brush. Leave for an hour and then buff with a soft shoe brush. The edge of the soft lambswool bonnet on your drill will also get into most nooks and crannies. Always use black or dark brown wax on carvings or you will inevitably be left with ugly white residue in at least one very visible nook.

When you have a protective wax coat in the depths of the carving, revert to polishing with a pad and polish the high surfaces only. Much of the beauty of carved oak comes from the contrast between the lighter, shinier surface and the darker, duller ground. The carvers knew this, which is why they often matted the background with a punch: respect their intent.

Problem Solving

If the surface has completely dried out or the wax has been cleaned off, follow the old craftsman's advice:

> Wax once a day for a week.
> Once a week for a month.
> Once a month for a year.
> And once a year for life.

If the surface has suffered a glossy refinish, rub it lightly and patiently with 0000 steel wool to reduce the worst of the gloss. Denatured alcohol on the wool can help. Work on a small area at a time, and wipe it with a paper towel as it dries. A slight white residue in the grain can be cleaned with the first coat of wax. Then, wax it once a day for a week ...

To clean furniture without disturbing the old wax surface under the grime, wash it with a pad of paper towels moistened with warm water and facial soap — do not use a harsh detergent such as one for washing dishes. An antique surface merits the same tender care as your complexion. Wash carefully, checking the pad to see the dirt that has come off. Continue until no more dirt appears on the pad, and then dry the wood with a soft cloth or paper towel. You can also use mineral spirits instead of soap and water. Wax the cleaned surface.

When a surface has become really grimy or has been neglected and dried out or worn unevenly, you may try to revive it. Mix equal parts of turpentine, methylated spirits or denatured alcohol, and raw linseed oil, shake it well, and apply it freely with a soft cloth, or, in bad cases, with 0000 steel wool. Wipe off the excess, leave it for a couple of days, and then wax.

White or black stains or rings are usually caused by moisture, alcohol, or oil penetrating the surface. If you are lucky, they will have gone no deeper than the polish. If this is the case, rub the stain with wax on 0000 steel wool. If this doesn't work, try one of the specially formulated "ring remover" products, or even a liquid metal polish. Rub very lightly, and very patiently, until the stain has gone, or has been greatly reduced. Then wax the whole surface.

If the stain has penetrated the wood, it will need bleaching and refinishing, a job best left to a professional. Or, unless it is really bad, do nothing. Black rings of about six inches in diameter have been left by a carelessly filled oil lamp a hundred or more years ago. They are common, almost irremoveable, and, in our opinion, not disfiguring. Just live with them — they are part of the history of the piece.

Wax scratches easily. Light scratches can be disguised with a commercial scratch remover or with a felt-tipped "touch up" pen of the right color. These pens will also color bare wood, such as an edge chip: scratch removers will not. Wipe off excess stain immediately.

If the color has been bleached out by sunlight, as has often happened with table tops, you have an aesthetic decision to make. If you dislike the look, remove the wax with denatured alcohol, stain the surface, and start building up a good wax finish again. Or ask a professional to do it for you. If, on the other hand, you like the contrast between the lighter horizontal surface and the darker vertical ones but wish it were not so extreme, use a mix of five parts turpentine to one part linseed oil to bring some of the color back. Then use black wax. Be patient. Wax it once a week for a long time. The color will return gradually, but never completely; the contrast will be muted, but always noticeable. What you will do with black wax, elbow grease, and patience is recover the figuring in the grain. Waxing is well worth the effort, but don't expect the impossible.

Finally, we need to dismiss some fairytales commonly told by advertisers who care only about selling products not about maintaining early oak furniture. Believe them at your peril. They are:

1. "Lemon" or "orange" oil is good because it "feeds" the wood. Wrong. Wood does not need oil, wood does not need feeding. These oils give a quick easy shine, but because they are kerosene (paraffin) based, in the long term they will damage an old finish. The "lemon" is merely an artificial scent masking the stink of paraffin.

2. Silicone (sprayed or wiped on) is good. Wrong. Another quick fix that damages. If you use silicone and you ever need to refinish your furniture, it will cause problems: even after stripping, its residue may prevent the new finish from adhering properly. Leave silicone for starlets' bosoms, where it does a fine job (apparently).

3. "Wax build-up" needs to be removed. Wrong. Wax "build-up" is patina: enough said!

If a product promises quick and easy results, don't use it. Patience, elbow grease, and wax are what early oak needs, and they are all that it needs.

Replacing Hardware

While some seventeenth-century pieces have kept their original hardware, you will find many where it has been replaced, or where it is missing and broken. Hinges and drawer-pulls are where you will meet the problem most frequently.

Hinges were made by the local blacksmith in iron, and, depending on his skill and the pocket of the owner, can take a number of forms: the snipe or cotter pin hinge is the cheapest and weakest. It is therefore prized when it survives. A stronger version of this is the strap-and-loop hinge. Both use the same principle: interlocked loops are fixed on the lid and the back of the chest. In the snipe hinge, the ends of the loop are inserted through the board and bent over like a modern cotter pin; in strap-and-loop hinges, the loops are on the end of straps that are nailed to the boards.

More expensive were hinges as we understand them today, where the two parts pivot on a hinge pin. They vary only in the shape of the iron flanges by which they are fixed to the boards: straps, butterflies and plain rectangles are the usual shapes.

Hinges were secured by nails, not screws. The square, tapering, blunt-ended shafts of handmade nails gripped oak as tightly as any screw and were far cheaper to make. On gate-leg tables, where the hinges carry a lot of weight, a rivet was occasionally used, though more frequently on continental furniture than on English.

If you need to replace iron hinges, take the time to find a company that makes accurate reproductions by hand. Or, better still, talk with a local blacksmith and see what he can do. You will only replace the hinges once, so do it right, and pay more than the local hardware store would charge you.

Drawers were opened either by wooden pulls or by drop handles of brass or iron. Few of either have survived. If you buy a piece whose pulls are later and stylistically inappropriate, you may choose to live with them if they have dulled and are not too jarring. But if you decide to replace them with appropriate reproductions, you will have to deal with the scars left by the pulls you remove. The holes will probably be in the wrong place, or will be two instead of one, and the surface under the back plate will be discolored. These problems are solvable, though they may need a professional restorer.

Then, follow the same advice as for hinges: get the best reproductions you can find. Find a company that makes cast brass pulls, not cheap pressed ones. For wooden pulls, you will probably do best to ask your restorer to turn new ones to fit the original holes.

Hasps and locks are often lost and are rarely worth replacing.

Finding a Restorer

There are three ways to look for a good restorer: the best, by far, is word of mouth.

Many good restorers have as much work as they can cope with and do not need to advertise: they rely on their existing customers and on word of mouth. Do not be surprised if your friendly dealer suddenly becomes less friendly when you ask him the name of his restorer. Dealers often guard their restorer jealously. This is partly because dealers like their restorers to be lean and hungry: the more work their restorer has, the longer they will have to wait before their piece is ready for sale. Another reason is the fear that you might see a piece in pieces before it returns to their shop in all its shining glory. They would prefer to tell you about the restoration than have you see the gory details for yourself.

Some dealers have their own restoration services that are available to the public. One of these is generally a safe choice: at the very least, you can see the quality of the work in the dealer's showroom.

Your local museum may be more forthcoming than your local dealer. The appropriate curator will usually know which of the local restorers does work that you can trust.

If word of mouth fails you, your other two resources are the internet and advertisements in the trade press (the restorer you want is unlikely to list himself in the yellow pages). The British Antique Furniture Restorers' Association (BAFRA) and the Antique Furniture Restorer's Fellowship both have good, searchable sites.

However you find a restorer, always visit his workshop and inspect examples of his work. Many will have a portfolio of their work that they will be happy to show you. And when you decide on him, be prepared to wait. The restorer you want will have a long backlog, and he is likely to give priority to dealers, because they are repeat customers.

Antiques as Investments

Buying an antique is not spending money: it is transferring your assets.

Early oak has proved a good investment for those who bought it well, and buying well means not buying it for its investment value! Buy it for its aesthetics, its authenticity, and its history, and it will almost certainly, in the long run, prove to be a good investment.

John Andrews has tracked the prices of antique furniture since 1968 for the British Antique Collectors Club (see Andrews 1989:40-67 and the journal *Antique Collecting*). The resulting index of antique furniture prices shows that a piece of furniture that cost £100 in 1968 would have cost £3575 in 2001: it would have increased by a factor of 35. For comparison, the London *Financial Times* Stock Index rose by a factor of 18 over the same period. On the face of it, antiques were twice as good an investment as stocks. They also performed slightly better than the house you put them in: average house prices in the southeast of England rose by a factor of 31 during the same time period.

More specifically, around the turn of the twenty-first century, early oak has risen in value faster than most other categories of antique furniture. It seems to be a good place to put your money, and, with one major proviso, it is.

Antiques are not liquid. Their selling costs are around 33% or higher, whereas those of houses are about 5%, and of shares 2% or less. The costs of selling an antique will eat up the first five years of its gain, so, financially, antiques are good only in the longer term. Ten years is the absolute minimum term for an antique to prove a good financial investment: longer is better.

Antiques are not like stocks: indeed, their investment value depends precisely upon their difference from stocks. People of taste want to live with their antiques over time. The low liquidity of an antique, therefore, is not a drawback, it is a built-in advantage. It may be difficult to imagine an investment whose appeal lies in its low liquidity, but that is what an antique is. If you love antiques, you necessarily have a long-term perspective, and that's the only perspective from which to view antiques as investments. If you want quick profits, stay out of antiques.

Good antiques are a good investment, they always have been, and they always will be. But they are good investments only because people of taste recognize and desire to own their beauty, their usefulness, their historical significance, and their rarity. And people of taste twenty years from now will, like you, want the best they can afford. The best antiques make the best investments. And, from our point of view, the best investments are the ones that we can appreciate while they are appreciating. Early oak fits the bill.

Glossary

Acanthus: Stylized leaves originally used in Greek and Roman architecture and frequently carved on English furniture from the sixteenth century to the present.

Anthemion: A stylized honeysuckle, Greek in origin, with narrow leaves or petals.

Arabesque: An intricate pattern of Arabic origin, disseminated via Spain (especially on tiles and pottery) and via Venice, by gilded leather bookbindings. Parisian bookbinders followed the Venetians, and the scholar Thomas Wotton was the first Englishman to send his books for binding in gold-tooled leather. The binding (c. 1548) on his copy of *Et Amicorum* is decorated with arabesques, strapwork, and other mannerist motifs (Thornton 1998:46).

Arcade: A semi-circular arch on pillars, or, commonly, a series of them.

Arcading: A series of arcades.

Arras: A Franco-Flemish town famous for producing wall hangings with interwoven threads of gold and silver — the value of which is the reason why almost none have survived. The town traded closely with England, importing raw wool and exporting tapestries. The word "arras" came to refer to tapestries in general, not just those produced in the town.

Atlas (pl. Atlantes): A male figure applied to furniture as a decorative support. Originally architectural (see Caryatid).

Aumbrey: An enclosed cupboard from the early seventeenth century and earlier. Generally, but not always, a food cupboard.

Bog oak: Oak that has lain in a peat bog and turned black. Used in inlay or for small objects. A native equivalent of ebony.

Caryatid: A female figure applied to furniture as a decorative support. Originally architectural. The word is sometimes used generically to include atlantes and terms.

Cupboard: Originally open shelves or boards for storage and display. Distinguished from a "press," which had doors. Frequently used in its modern, not its original, sense.

Deal: The English craftsman's term for soft woods imported from the Baltic or northern Europe. There is no deal tree. Deal may be pine, spruce, or fir. Soft-wood trees did not grow in England in the seventeenth century.

Dormant: A piece of furniture, usually a long table, that is constructed in one piece and is not intended to be dismantled after each use.

"Feete": The seventeenth-century word for legs.

Fleur de Lys (England) or **Lis** (U.S.): A three-petaled lily, deriving from the Egyptian lotus, the heraldic device of the Bourbons of France, widely used as a decorative motif across Europe.

Fluting: Vertical concave channels on pillars and pilasters; the opposite of "reeding."

Gadrooning: A series of short convex lobes, sometimes tapering into teardrops, often used as a border decoration.

Guilloche: A series of circles run together. Originally Greek, popularized by Serlio.

Inlay: wood of a contrasting color that is set into the surface for decorative purposes.

"Jacobethan": A recently-coined word that Timothy Mowl (1993:195) borrowed from John Betjeman's *Ghastly Good Taste* (1933) to refer to the period from Queen Elizabeth I to Charles I (1558-1648). It usefully implies that the style-period was coherent and that the changes of monarch were not accompanied by significant changes in style, unlike, say, the change between Jacobethan and Restoration, or between William and Mary and Queen Anne. The word can be used straightfacedly to refer to the original style and period and more satirically to refer the "Jacobethan" revival in the nineteenth century. Betjeman's original coinage was satirical. Now, however, particularly among architects, Jacobethan is becoming the name of choice for the revival style. It is also used to identify the mass-produced furniture popular between the two world wars. This book follows Mowl in using the word descriptively, and not satirically, and in using it to refer to the period and not a revival.

Linenfold: A carved representation, usually on a panel, of the folds of hanging fabric.

Livery: Food, usually bread, cheese, and beer, that was given to members of the household to sustain them beyond the main meal of the day. Livery was generally eaten before sleeping and upon awakening. The word was used to describe the small ventilated cupboards that stored livery, and later, the household uniforms of the retainers that were eligible to receive it.

Lotus: An Egyptian motif of a bud with a stylized leaf on each side, sometimes of three leaves.

Lozenge: A diamond shape that is usually filled with another motif.

Lunette: A semi-circle, usually arched upwards, often filled with another motif and often in an interlaced series.

Marquetry: Veneered designs applied to the surface and not inlaid into it. Popular in the late seventeenth century.

Molding: A decoration of straight lines or grooves cut into the surface using a molding plane or chisel. Also a strip of wood, profiled with a molding plane, that is applied to the surface, often in geometric patterns.

Nulling: A series of concave niches with rounded tops and square bases. Architectural in origin.

Ogee: A double- or S-curved molding, usually convex over concave.

Ovolo: A quarter-round molding, often around the edges of joint stools or tables. The top of the molding is stepped down from the main surface. Sometimes called "thumbnail."

Palmette, or **Palmate**: leafy decoration, often almost semi-circular, sometimes elongated like a palm leaf. Assyrian, Egyptian, and Greek in origin.

Period: The time-span within which a style originated and was first popular. Used to differentiate the original period from a revival.

Pilgrim century: An American furniture period from the early seventeenth century to c. 1735, when it is succeeded by the Queen Anne and Colonial periods. It ends with the William and Mary style. In American usage, the names of English monarchs are given to the styles that characterize their reigns and do not, as in England, refer to the dates when they reigned. The American Queen Anne period begins c. 1735, long after the lady herself had died.

Press: An enclosed cupboard.

Quatrefoil: Four leaves joined at the center by their stems.

Reeding: Vertical convex ridges on pillars and pilasters, resembling a bundle of reeds. The opposite of fluting.

Romayne: A Renaissance decoration of a profile head in a roundel, usually on a panel, surrounded by mannerist motifs. The inspiration came from Roman coins. The Venetian engraver Enea Vico published portraits of the Caesars' wives in 1557 (and later of the Caesars) that he copied from Roman coins. The English name "Romayne" means Roman.

Rose, Rosette, Roseace: A stylized rose, originally Egyptian but popular from the Tudor period onward. An emblem of the Tudor monarchs, but not always.

Seeled, or sealed: a seeled room was one lined with wainscot paneling — the term is the origin of "ceiling."

Spandrel: The space between the corner of a square frame and a circular design inside it.

Term: In Roman times, a carved figure set in the ground to mark the terminal point of a piece of property. In mannerism, an applied figure, similar to a caryatid, but not acting as a support. Sometimes used generically to refer to any applied figure whether caryatid, atlas, or term.

Thumbnail: See ovolo.

Trefoil: Three leaves joined at the center by their stems.

Trencher: A square of stale bread used as a plate in the Middle Ages. A plate, usually wooden, for individual use. A small salt cellar used by one or two diners. The word indicates individual rather than communal use at the table.

Wainscot: Oak imported from the Baltic, particularly Denmark. Its high quality, quarter-sawn boards were cut from large, straight, slow-grown trees. Compared to native oak, it had fewer knots and straighter grain; it was lighter in weight, paler in color, and lower in tannin; it was less liable to warp and could be cut more thinly without sacrificing strength. It was ideally suited for panels. Wainscot was used by better joiners for more expensive pieces, particularly in the south. Conversely, native oak was cheaper, and its use is often a sign of provincial origin. Native oak was mainly used for construction, both of buildings and ships, but was also used for furniture. The tannin in oak attacks iron, so oak furniture was pegged rather than nailed. The dark tannin stain around any nails or hinges is less marked on wainscot than on native oak. The word "wainscot" may derive from the German *wandtschott*, meaning "wall boarding," or from the Dutch *wagenschott*, meaning "wagon shaft." Today it is commonly used to refer to anything made with panels, particularly chairs and wall-paneling, though not, oddly, coffers.

References

Andrews, John (1989). *British Antique Furniture: Price Guide and Reasons for Values.* Woodbridge, Antique Collectors' Club. A useful general guide, with comprehensive illustrations, and a good section on Victorian carve-ups.

Andrews, John (1997). *Antique Furniture.* Woodbridge, Antique Collectors' Club. An introductory book whose first three chapters usefully survey European furniture up to the end of the seventeenth century.

Bebb, Richard (1994). *Welsh Country Furniture.* Princes Risborough, Shire Publications. A brief and interesting survey.

Bowett, Adam (2002). *English Furniture 1660-1714: From Charles II to Queen Ann,* Woodbridge, the Antique Collectors' Club. Focused mainly on high-style walnut furniture, but includes some oak. Particularly good on the Great Fire of London's impact on the furniture industry. Highly recommended.

Chinnery, Victor (1979). *Oak Furniture, the British Tradition,* Woodbridge, the Antique Collectors' Club. The definitive work, scholarly, comprehensive, and very well illustrated. The appendices are the only place where long extracts from Randle Holme and William Harrison are easily available. Every collector should own a copy.

Cullity, Brian (1994). *A Cubbered, Four Joyne Stools & Other Smalle Thinges: The Material Culture of Plymouth Colony,* Catalog of a loan exhibition, the Heritage Plantation of Sandwich, Massachusetts.

Edwards, Clive (2000). *Encyclopedia of Furniture Materials, Trades and Techniques.* Aldershot, Ashgate Publishing.

Edwards, Ralph (1964). *The Shorter Dictionary of English Furniture,* London, Hamlyn. The great, classic reference book that covers early furniture particularly well. Highly recommended. Reissued by the Antique Collectors' Club.

Edwards, Ralph and Ramsey, L. G. G. (eds.) (1968). *The Connoisseur's Complete Period Guides to the Houses, Decoration, Furnishing and Chattels of the Classic Periods,* New York, Bonanza Books.

Elias, Norbert (1978). *The Civilizing Process: the Development of Manners*, New York, Urizen Books.

Fastnedge, Ralph (1955). *English Furniture Styles 1500-1830*, Harmondsworth and Baltimore, Penguin Books.

Forman, Benno M. (1988). *American Seating Furniture 1630-1730*, New York and London, Norton. Helpfully explores the common roots of American and English furniture.

Knell, David (1992). *English Country Furniture: The Vernacular Tradition 1500-1900*, Woodbridge, the Antique Collectors' Club. Contains good examples and very good contextual background for early furniture, and traces its development in English country furniture. Highly recommended.

Little, Nina Fletcher (2001). *Neat & Tidy: Boxes and Their Contents Used in Early American Households*, The Society for the Preservation of New England Antiquities.

MacQuoid, Percy (1904). *The Age of Oak*, London, Lawrence and Bullen. An early classic, still useful to the more advanced collector.

Mowl, Timothy (1993). *Elizabethan & Jacobean Style*, London, Phaidon Press. An engagingly well written and beautifully illustrated architect's account of the taste of the period. Focused on the houses (both inside and out) in which the furniture was placed. Good background reading.

Nutting, Wallace (1921). *Furniture of the Pilgrim Century 1620-1720*, New York, Bonanza Books.

Quiney, Anthony (1990). *The Traditional Buildings of England*, London, Thames and Hudson.

Rumble, Penny (1993). *Carved Decoration on Early English Woodwork*, Wolverhampton, Turner Press.

Rybczynski, Witold (1986). *Home, a Short History of an Idea*, New York, Viking Books.

Thornton, Peter (1998). *Form and Decoration: Innovation in the Decorative Arts 1470-1870*. London, Weidenfield and Nicolson; New York, Abrams.

Trent, Robert, "Furniture in the New World: The Seventeenth Century," in

Gerald Ward (ed.) (1991). *American Furniture with Related Decorative Arts, 1660-1830*, New York, Hudson Hills Press.

Wills, Geoffrey (1971). *English Furniture 1550-1760*, London, Guiness Superlatives.

Wolsey, S. M. and Luff, R. W. P. (1969). *Furniture in England: The Age of the Joiner*, New York and Washington, Praeger.

Sources from the Period

William Harrison, A *Description of England, or a brief rehearsal of the nature and qualities of the people of England and such commodities as are to be found in the same.* First published in 1577, and in 1587 published with Holinshed's *Chronicle.* William Harrison (1534-93) was the Rector of Radwinter and Canon of Windsor.

Randle Holme, *The Academy of Armory, or, a Storehouse of Blazonry*, published in 1688, but the manuscript is dated 1649 when Holme completed his "first colleccions and draughts" for the work. The work was republished by the Roxburghe Club in 1905. Holme was primarily concerned with heraldry, but he included accounts of the houses and furnishings typical of the families whose heraldic devices he studied.

Samuel Pepys wrote his famous diaries in a shorthand code during the first decade of the Restoration, 1660-1669. The diaries were discovered, decoded, and published in 1825. They are available on line at www.pepysdiary.com.

Recommended for Your Personal Reference Library

Chinnery (1997) is a must. Add Knell (1992) and you have the two most immediately useful reference books. As your interest develops, buy Edwards (1964), Bowett (2002), and Mowl (1993). Andrews (1989) sets early oak in a longer perspective. For American furniture, add Forman (1988), and of course, Nutting (1921). Add the others in this list as and when you find them: many are out of print.

Index

acanthus 39, 47, 48, 193
American 26, 50-53, 87, 96, 105,
    109-10, 113-15, 143, 183
Andrews, John 177, 190, 197, 199
anthemion 193
apprentice, apprenticeship 25, 54,
    143
arabesque 47, 48, 154, 193
arcade, arch 48, 57, 154, 193
architecture, architectural 38, 40-1,
    42, 43, 46, 48, 50, 55, 57, 136,
    149
ark 79-80
arras 7, 12, 152, 153, 193
Atlas (Atlantes) 39, 40-1, 43, 46, 193,
    194
Aumbrey (almery) 81, 82, 83, 193

backstool. *See* chair
Bebb, Richard 108, 197
bed 13, 16, 17, 19, 28, 149-59
  bedding 150, 152, 153
  bedstaff, bedstaves 151, 152, 155
  bedstock 152, 157
  bedstuff 150-2, 157
  half-headed 156-7
  headboard, bedhead 16, 153-4
  tester 135, 151, 153-7
  truckle, trundle 151, 157-8
bench. *See* form
boarded 22, 30, 104
Bowett, Adam 97, 99, 197, 199
box
  bible 18, 28, 52, 179
  desk 63, 64

cabinet-maker, cabinet-making 23,
    33, 55, 98

candlestand 130-2
capital 11, 43, 136
carpenter 22, 27, 28-9, 104
carpet 5, 13, 120, 153
carver 28, 37, 39, 42-56
carving
  chip 45
  figural 46, 50
  gouge 45, 46
  relief 45-6, 49, 50
  scratch 45, 46, 51, 175-7
  sunk or flat 45, 46, 51, 176
carve-up 175-80
caryatid 16, 38, 39, 40-2, 43, 46, 50,
    193
chair 3, 8-10, 12, 15, 28, 104
  backstool 3, 14, 15, 89, 93, 96-103,
    121, 168-9
  caned 15, 34, 96-9, 104
  Cromwellian 53, 54, 99, 100
  turner's, turned 106, 110-15
  wainscot or great 8, 91-6, 99, 106,
    109, 135, 166, 170, 178
Charles II 33, 34, 35
chest. *See* coffer
chest of drawers 68-9
  enclosed 54, 55-7, 70, 73
Chinnery, Victor xv, 52, 105, 133,
    150, 180, 197, 199
clamped front 79-80
coffer or chest 17-18, 27, 30, 50, 51,
    65-9, 93, 106, 154, 166, 175
Cromwell 13, 35, 37, 40, 53-5, 99-
    100, 121, 135, 139
cup-and-cover 6, 11, 88, 119, 136
Chippendale 173, 174
Cullity, Brian, 197
cupboard 194

court 4, 5, 6, 9, 10-13, 135-41, 153, 167
dole 81, 84
glass 84, 86
livery 31, 80-4, 179
press 43, 74-9, 139, 140, 194, 195
spice 84-5
standing 76
standing livery 82, 137-42

deal, 26, 194
display 10-13, 135-39, 142, 150
dovetail. *See* joint
dragon (sea serpent) 42, 47, 56
dresser 141-7
  high 145, 147
  low 13, 14, 55, 141-7
  Welsh 145, 147

Edwards, Ralph 42, 118, 151, 185, 197, 199
Elizabethan 3, 4, 5, 7, 8, 12, 16, 17, 24, 35, 37-8, 39, 40, 42, 43, 50, 54-5, 93, 99, 113, 119, 127, 133, 136, 143, 149, 153, 161, 178, 182
Erasmus 10, 17, 19, 20
Evelyn, John 118, 185

Fastnedge, Ralph 198
feet 10, 110, 131, 167
  bun 72, 74
  shoe 106
  stile 72-4
fleur-de-lys 194
floor 10, 88, 132, 167
foliage, foliate 47, 48, 50
form or bench 3, 4, 9, 12, 14, 27, 103-6, 169
Forman, Benno 52, 96, 105, 110, 198, 199

gadroon 47, 49, 50, 136, 194

geometry, geometric 49, 50, 54-7
gothic 44, 173-80
grape-and-vine 39, 45, 47, 48, 50, 56
Great Bed of Ware 16, 17, 149, 151, 155
Great Fire of London 34, 35
guild 22-36, 39, 143
guilloches 40, 43, 47-50, 154, 194

hangings 16, 152, 154, 157
Harrison, William 7, 11, 152-3, 199
Henry VIII 25, 37, 120, 143
Hentzner, Paul 10, 149
hierarchy 3, 6-7, 8, 15, 91
hinge 123, 124, 189
Holme, Randle 87, 93, 103-4, 110, 113, 120, 131, 135, 151, 152, 199

individual 3, 14-21, 105, 161
inlay 38, 43, 46, 50, 76, 194
investment 190-1

Jacobean 3, 8, 16, 35, 37, 55, 99
Jacobethan 37-8, 42, 46-7, 50, 125, 142, 150, 153, 176, 194
Japanning 98-99
joiner, joyner xiv-xv, 22, 27-29, 30, 33, 34, 36, 39, 55, 98, 113
joint, joined 22, 45
  dovetail 22, 28, 29, 33, 34, 130
  mortise-and-tenon xiv-xv, 23, 28, 33, 99, 113
  rule 123
  tongue-and-groove 122, 123, 124
journeyman 25

Knell, David 141, 198

Lemnus, Levinus 10
linenfold 44, 66, 194
Little, Nina Fletcher 61, 198
livery 12, 80-2, 137, 140, 142, 194-5

looking-glass 152, 160-1
loss 169, 170-1
Louden, J.C. 174, 177
lozenge 49, 56, 94, 95, 154, 175, 195
lunette 46, 48-50, 175, 195

Mannerism, Mannerist 37-44, 54-6,
       106, 142
marquetry 34, 55, 127, 195
medieval, Middle Ages 16, 18, 19-21,
       24, 26, 35, 37, 39, 42, 93, 113,
       133, 152, 161, 174
melon, see also cup-and-cover 11, 136
modern 3, 21, 161
molding 79, 195
   channel-and-groove 45, 46, 176
   dentil 57
   geometric 54, 55, 57, 71-2, 78
Mowl, Timothy 18, 42, 43, 198, 199
mule chest 56, 71

nulling 47, 48, 50, 195
Nutting, Wallace 110, 198, 199

panel, paneling xv, 27, 42, 43, 44, 45
palmette 46-8, 195
Parchemin 44
patina 182-4
Pepys, Samuel 15, 33, 89, 120, 124,
       158, 199
portrait 14, 20, 161
private, privacy 13-18, 96, 149-50,
       158
provenance 181-2

quatrefoil 47, 49
Quinney, Anthony 26, 198

rank (social) 7, 9, 13, 14, 90, 106
Renaissance 38, 40, 44, 55, 180, 182
renaming 179
repair 165-71
replacement 89-90, 103, 165-71, 188-9

reproduction 179
Restoration (of the monarchy) 10, 13,
       14, 35, 54-7, 94, 97, 125, 131,
       141, 153
restoration 89-90, 103, 124, 127, 141,
       147, 159, 165-71, 182, 189-90
Romayne 44, 47, 49, 50, 195
roseace, rose 43, 49, 195
Rumble, Penny 39, 198

salt 7, 20
   master 7, 14
   trencher 7, 14
Searle, William 52, 96
Serlio, Sebastian 55, 177
settle 106-10
Shakespeare, William 6, 20, 149
spindle, split 50
status 4, 14, 15, 93, 94, 105, 113, 117
stool 3, 8-10, 14, 28, 91
   boarded 87
   box 91
   close 90
   joint 4, 6, 28, 30, 86-92, 99, 104-5,
       125, 179, 183
   turned 20, 87, 110, 133
strapwork 40, 47, 50, 136, 154
stretcher xv, 4, 6, 10, 88, 119, 121,
       123, 127, 144, 167, 169, 190

table 13, 28, 88
   altar 133
   center 129
   coaching 129
   credence or folding 14, 126-7, 179
   cricket 131-3
   dormant 6, 117, 120
   gate-leg, oval, round 5, 7, 10, 14-15,
       20, 96, 103, 122-5, 161, 179
   high 12
   long, refectory 3, 5-8, 10, 12, 14,
       20, 86, 105, 117-22, 136, 179
   serving 20, 133, 145

side 127-9
trestle 5, 7, 12, 20, 117-18, 119
withdrawing 6, 119
writing 128-9
tapestry 5, 7, 13
term 194, 196
textiles 5, 150
throw, throwing 30, 110
trencher 8, 20, 196
Trent, Robert 198-9
tulip 48, 51, 52, 56
turned, turner 22, 27, 29-33, 39, 54,
        110, 113, 130
turning
  baluster 55, 145
  barrel 89
  bobbin 54, 55, 127-8, 132
  spiral 54, 100, 123, 127, 131, 132
  vase 89, 127, 128, 132
Tuscany, Duke of 15, 90-91

upholder, upholsterer 33-5, 94, 95

veneer 22, 33, 34, 128, 132
Victorian 41, 89, 110, 120, 126, 133,
        141, 173-80
wainscot 7, 12, 26, 196
Walpole, Horace 113, 173, 174
wax, waxing 183, 185-8
William and Mary 3, 88, 96, 143,
        145
Wills, Geoffrey 199
Wolsey, S.M., and Luff, R.W.P. 105,
        199